GW00372061

Glen Fender Meadows

A Celebration of Diversity

Glen Fender Meadows

A Celebration of Diversity

in the company of
John Ford

Dedications

To the memory of
Joy
and those so special days spent
botanizing on 'our meadow'.

To John and Janet
for their Highland welcome
and friendship over the years.

Published in 2012 by John Ford

Copyright © John Ford
All rights reserved

No part of this book may be reproduced, stored in a retrieval system or transmitted in
any form or by any means without the prior written permission of the copyright holder.

ISBN 978-0-9573433-0-6

Printed and bound by Shanleys, The Stables, Levens Hall, Cumbria LA8 0PB,
using FSC approved paper and vegetable-based inks.

Contents

Page

vi   Foreword

vii   Acknowledgements

ix   Preface
      Setting the Scene

15   Prologue

17   Spring: first signs
      to full awakening
      (latc April - May)

49   Mid Summer
      (June)

97   High Summer
      (July)

159 A time of transition
      (August)

191 Autumn: bright colours
      and fruitfulness
      (September and October)

211 The winter months
      (November to March)

219 Epilogue

222 Appendices:
      A) Scientific names for the illustrated flowering plants
      B) Scientific names for the flowering plant families encountered
      C) Sources of Information

Foreword

I first new John Ford and Joy Wilcox (soon to become Mrs Ford) when we were all undergraduates reading Botany at the University of Hull in the early 1960s. We were taught by an inspiring group of lecturers, led by Professor Noel Robertson, and shared with them a passion for plants that has stayed with us all our lives. Sadly, Joy died in 2008, but her passion for plants lives on in this book, which is a most fittingly dedicated to her memory.

Meanwhile, another of John's consuming interests was photographing plants and other wildlife, an interest he still pursues with an enthusiast's zeal and a professional's skill. For him nothing but perfection is good enough and I have many memories of waiting, not always patiently, on rain-swept moors or sun-drenched sand-dunes, whilst he completed a shot of a particular plant to his complete satisfaction. Soon after moving to Scotland, John and Joy 'discovered' by chance the species-rich Highland meadow that is the subject of this book. It was inevitable from the start that they would return to it countless times through the seasons and over the years, with John recording all they saw with his camera. The visual feast to be found in the pages that follow is testimony both to John and Joy's shared love of the natural world and to John's relentless quest for perfection as a photographer.

John invites the reader to think of the meadow as a canvas "on which nature 'paints' an ever changing picture as the seasons progress and merge one into another". Naturally, plants are at the heart of the book, but the mammals, birds, butterflies and other insects drawn to this rich habitat were not allowed to escape John's all-seeing lens. The reader is drawn, almost imperceptibly, into an awareness of their physical presence: at first, it seems, 'out of the corner of and eye' and then, through a leap of imagination, into 'hearing the evocative sounds they add to the sigh of the ever-present wind. From time to time throughout the book John digresses in the text from the simple but highly informative descriptions that accompany all his photographs and presents us, instead, with a brief vignette that offers an insight into one or other of the many and complex ways in which plants and animals co-exist with the environment. A valuable bibliography then provides the perfect starting point for any reader wishing to explore these relationships further.

Many of John's friends, including myself, have tried over the years to persuade him to publish a selection of his photographs of the meadow, arguing that they were too interesting and valuable to remain hidden away from the world. For various reasons John resisted our entreaties. Now, however, he has given-in and has produced this unique and wonderful book. I am so pleased that he has done so, for it will give immense pleasure to all who read it. Moreover, whilst it is not possible to predict the effects on the meadow of environmental changes and evolving farming practices over the coming decades, John's book will stand for ever as an invaluable testimony to an inspiring example of the way in which agriculture and the natural world may co-exist in harmony.

David Ingram, OBE, VMH, ScD, FRSE
Honorary Professor, Edinburgh and Lancaster Universities; formerly Regius Keeper, the Royal Botanic Garden Edinburgh and then Master, St Catharine's College, Cambridge.

Acknowledgements

I am greatly indebted to the following people for their interest, encouragement and help, in various ways:

John Cameron, Brian Coppins, Mike Hay, Ros Hay, Alison Ingram, Phil Lusby, David Poyce, Barbara Richardson, Mike Richardson, David Sales, Mark Simmens, John Tinning.

I owe a particular debt of gratitude to Prof. David Ingram for the unstinting use of his own time to provide me with perceptive comments and suggestions regarding the text. Also, from the outset, a gentle push when my impetus flagged.

I must emphasise, however, that the content of this book is solely my responsibility and I sincerely hope that any errors will not detract from the primary objective - to celebrate the diversity of the meadow.

Author's note

Having viewed this site intermittently over a number of years I have become aware of apparent subtle changes. For example, globeflowers seem reduced in numbers, as do curlews. With all environments it is difficult to tell whether changes are short term and cyclical, or longer term continuous trends. To distinguish between the two requires rigorous scientific analysis - my observations are purely subjective. Yet looking at the wider environment there is compelling evidence that long term changes, due to such factors as climate change, are occurring. Obviously the meadow cannot escape the effects of such factors, as well as being influenced by any local changes. In putting this book together it is my earnest hope that it will provide an interesting archive of the meadow relevant to a particular time span.

Over the years I have visited many different locations, having been told about them. I am always conscious that other people may well do the same, with the potential to cause a detrimental impact. However, one feature of the meadow that has drawn me back over the years is that so much can be seen at or from the roadside and a vehicular track. Of the ninety five flowering plant species illustrated, eighty three of them can be seen at or from the roadside and seventy five were also photographed at the roadside or within approximately twenty five meters of it.

The meadow in full bloom and full sun

Preface
Setting the Scene

When I reflect on my journey through this life I find it surprising how decisions made in a moment of time can so often be salutary in their outcome. So it was in 1977 when my wife Joy and I, plus our then two small boys, were camping in Perthshire. We had to be off the site by noon but as it was a beautiful sunny June day, rather than head for home straight away, we decided to explore for a while. A road was chosen that seemed quite flat initially but then started climbing and finally finished up on a meadow. The difference in temperature between the bottom of the valley and where we were (about 300 m) was such that the boys would not get out of the car! However, we explored for about half an hour and in that time noted over forty species of flowering plants. A few years later in 1983, when our offspring were starting to be independent, we decided to make a return trip which in the event turned out to be the first of many. I took a camera with me and photographed plants close to the road. Eventually, in 1985, I approached a farmer to explain what I was up to and ask if I might explore more widely (the meadow covers approximately 100 hectares), mindful of vulnerable plant areas, like flushes, and that activity would need to be restricted during the nesting season. Permission was readily granted and so began a project which I pursued as and when time permitted. Joy, an enthusiastic botanist, frequently came with me and was a great help when it came to identifying the plants. Visits of one or sometimes two days were made about twice a month on average, between mid-May and August, but were rather spasmodic at other times of the year. This pattern of activity continued until 2006 and the text relates to observations made spanning these years. My photographic endeavours, carried out in very varied weather conditions, have provided a record of many of the flowering plants present on the meadow. A selection of these has been used to illustrate this book, along with non-flowering plants, fungi and animals. Except for the photograph of a plant we see on a detour, one or two high magnification macro-photographs (for which plant material was removed) and a photograph of the nearby large loch, all other photographs were taken on or from the meadow.

More meadow flowers - on a dull day

Mountain Pansies

The apparent floristic richness that attracted us both to the area in the first place has over the years proved to have been no illusion. There would seem to be a number of factors that contribute to this. One is the elevation, roughly between 280 and 350 m. The difference in temperature between the valley and the meadow that we noticed on our first visit was not a one-off experience but something that we were often to be made aware of. In addition the wind speed could be noticeably greater. Also, there has been an infiltration into the meadow flora of some plants that are associated with hilly/montane regions as, for example, the mountain pansy. Another factor is the topography. The ground slopes downwards from a road to a river and is markedly undulating. Most of this can be categorized as meadow grassland in which are interspersed distinctive features. There are some quite obvious protuberances that I will refer to as knolls. Water seems to run off these quite readily. In places water drains down towards the river in flushes which provide areas that are permanently wet. There are also depressions that retain water, creating distinctly boggy conditions. The effect of these circumstances is that the soil available for plant growth can vary from permanently waterlogged to relatively dry.

Some of the flowering plants, such as wood anemone, may be regarded as woodland species. Whilst trees are present, quite commonly the woodland plants are found growing in parts of the meadow devoid of trees, sometimes quite profusely. However, there are tree stumps present in some places. Enquiries have led me to understand that at least some of these trees were cut down during the last war, but that the area was lightly wooded before that, rather than being a woodland as such. Nevertheless this may account, at least in part, for the presence of woodland species. Along with the trees currently on the meadow, there are local plantations of Scots pine that juxtapose with some edges of the meadow.

Wood Anemones

Whilst not detracting from the influences so far mentioned, the meadow would not be as it is if it were not for the critically important fact that it has been farmed in a traditional Highland manner. It is not cut for hay, but cattle and sheep graze the area over winter. This prevents the vegetation from become rank and excluding light from herbaceous plants, especially, during the growing season. Most of the animals are taken off the meadow in the 'summer period' and moved to somewhat higher ground closer to the foothills of the mountains. The meadow is then only lightly grazed. This gives flowering plants the opportunity for sustained growth, flowering and setting seed/storing food before the animals return. So as is the case for meadows in general, this area is not a natural habitat but rather one maintained by and dependent upon a particular farming practice.

Regarding the photography, I started out with a 35 mm single lens reflex camera, a 50 mm macro lens and two flash guns. Some time later I added a wide angle lens to the outfit. Initially I used the flashguns a great deal as the short duration of a flash ensured a blur free image when there was a wind, which was frequently the situation. However, I soon became dissatisfied with the dark unnatural backgrounds due to the fall off in the flash light intensity with distance. It was not too long before I abandoned flash altogether and relied solely on whatever natural light was available. Wind then became a major problem, with having to wait for a lull to take a shot. Lulls were often of very short duration and then there was a nagging doubt that the subject was still enough when the shutter was pressed to have avoided a blurred image. So, I would wait for another lull and possibly another to try to ensure a sharp image! This process involved remaining relatively still for quite a time. However, the bonus was that one became accepted as part of the landscape by animals. One occasion that is for ever etched in my memory is when I heard a noise behind me that I took to be Joy returning from botanizing further away. As I turned round and said "How have you got on?", I found myself staring at a roe deer eyeball to eyeball.

It was not long after this that I decided to diversify to include animals as well as non-flowering plants and fungi. I invested in a second camera body and a telephoto lens. I always had this outfit by my side ready for possible action whilst engaged in photographing plants. Later, I also bought a more powerful telephoto lens that gave me more 'reach', but was distinctly heavier than my original purchase. This I commonly used resting on the sill of the car window; the access road conveniently ran more or less along one edge of the meadow. Over the years I have used a variety of film stock and then two years ago I decided to embrace digital technology. This brought with it two advantages. First, I was able to check immediately if a flower was sharp or blurred; a great saving of time. Second, it was possible to get acceptable photographs at lower light levels than with film and so extend the working day. In producing this book all my film transparencies have been scanned. Some film types seemed to produce acceptable scans more readily than others; 'Kodachrome' in particular, proved to be difficult which was unfortunate since for many years I had used this exclusively.

Another encounter

I am not sure who was more surprised but this time I was prepared!

As this book is in no way a scientific treatise vernacular names have been used for the most part. Those for flowering plants have been taken from the 2007 data base list of common names provided by the Botanical Society of the British Isles. The common names for fungi have been taken from a list produced by the Fungus Conservation Forum.

When I give talks two questions relating to the flowering plants are commonly asked: 'Do some plants prefer a particular type of soil; and, 'Looking at the diversity, how many plant families are represented'? The answer to the first question is that at least some do. Most of the plants are found in areas where observation would suggest that there is moderate drainage. However, several found on the knolls have a definite preference for drier areas and likewise there are those growing in waterlogged and damp areas that are not found elsewhere. Also, examination of the species list reveals another facet of the nature of the soil in that preferences range from acidic to base-rich (alkaline) soils. In this context I have commonly noted in the text which species seems to prefer either an acidic or a base-rich soil. Where there is no comment, it may be assumed that a particular species is usually associated with neutral soil. With regard to the second question, I have also stated for each species the family to which it belongs; so as we meander through the meadow you will be able to keep a tally if you wish!

Purple Milk-vetch:
associated with base-rich soil

Bilberry:
associated with acid soil

Prologue

This brown hare was my first mammal photograph on the meadow. It was April, the air was damp and chill. The presence of snow on the distant hills indicates that the demise of winter is a slow process. As the hare surveys the bleak landscape we can imagine this as the canvas on which nature will paint an ever changing picture of plants and fungi. As our excursion progresses over the next twelve months we will observe the plants and fungi that contribute to these changes. Also, we will come across many of the animals that interact with the meadow for some or all of the time.

Brown Hare

Spring: first signs to full awakening
(late April - May)

Creeping Willow

[willow family]

Patches of this ground-hugging, creeping pussy willow are not particularly obvious until one gets fairly close, when the bright yellow pollen on the male flowers attract the attention. Male and female flowers (catkins) occur on separate plants. The flowers of both sexes possess nectaries which provide a valuable food source for early insects.

Male catkins with feeding **Dung fly**

The female catkins, in contrast, blend in with the habitat and may be overlooked. Their presence becomes more obvious, however, when they produce seeds, as will be seen in due course.

Colt's-foot

[daisy family]

A quite familiar plant to be seen is the colt's-foot. Its sudden appearance is another indicator that spring is on the away. In this locality it seems to favour heavy damp ground, if not on the river bank then fairly close to it. The large leaves appear after the flowers have seeded and died back and have, perhaps fancifully, been likened to the shape of the foot of a young horse or a colt. We will come across them later.

Common Dog-violet

[violet family]

Common dog-violets occur quite widely. The blue-violet flowers make a welcome addition to the flora at this time, even though the term 'dog' is used by botanists to indicate a species that is thought to be inferior to some of its relatives!

The large number of plants growing close together make quite a splash of colour.

Wood Anemone

[buttercup family]

It is usual to think of these as woodland plants which complete their life cycles before the surrounding trees leaf out and cast shade on the woodland floor. Trees grew on this land long ago, although the cover was probably not extensive. Whether these wood anemones had their origins in that long-lost woodland is not known, but however they came to inhabit the meadow, they now grow over quite extensive areas of open ground.

Their flower heads, which bob so daintily in the wind, seem to appear almost overnight.

When looking at plants there is always the chance of coming across something else of interest.

This tussock of vegetation, for example, is used by a brown hare to back into and so gain some protection from the elements. Such hideaways, which also make the hare less visible to its enemies, are known as 'forms'.

Primrose

[primrose family]

Primroses are not very plentiful on the meadow and are limited to a few widely separate sites, which are damp and shaded from strong sunlight for at least part of the day. Nevertheless, they do appear consistently from year to year and are always a pleasure to find.

To most people it is the primrose, with its flowers growing from the middle of an attractive rosette of leaves, that really marks the beginning of spring rather than the colt's-foot which actually appears earlier.

The name for the plant derives from two Latin words, *prima* and *rosa,* meaning 'first rose'.

Wood-sorrel

[wood-sorrel family]

This diminutive plant is found in a similar, though slightly more shaded habitat, to that of the primroses.

Cowslip

[primrose family]

This name derives from the Old English 'cuslyppe' or what we would now most likely call a cowpat. Indeed in traditional meadows cowslips are often found in close proximity to cowpats.

Cowslips are another example of the yellow spring flowers with distinctive drooping flower heads of flowers that are smaller than those of the primrose. They do not appear on the meadow in any great number, nor with certainty every year, but are always associated with base-rich soil.

Bitter-vetch

[pea family]

Bitter-vetch is the first member of the pea family to put in an appearance and is clearly quite at home in hilly areas especially where the soil tends to be acidic. As it lacks tendrils it is low growing and spreads by means of creeping stems. The flowers are a distinctive reddish purple colour at first, but as they age this fades to blue then green. The tubers of this plant have in the past been dried and kept to be eaten to ward off hunger when required. Also, they have been used as a flavouring both in food and whisky.

Water Avens

[rose family]

Water avens has characteristic drooping flowers and is found in damper areas. This plant was photographed at the base of a drystane dyke where a small damp ditch had formed. When the seed heads mature they are covered in small hooks – a natural form of 'Velcro' as they readily attach themselves to any passing animal with a 'woolly' coat.

Looking at the close up photograph of a drooping flower head it is easy to see how the popular name of 'grandma's bonnet' originated.

Mountain Everlasting

[daisy family]

This is one of a number of plants found on the meadow which have a name suggesting an association with hilly areas. On the meadow it grows in some of the drier places, especially the sloping side of a knoll.

Male and female flowers occur on separate plants, the female are a rose pink colour and the male vary from pink to pure white. Bracts, structures that surround a flower head, are petal shaped in male plants and in female plants they are numerous and fine, giving a flower head a wooly appearance.

Male plants

Female plants

They look like diminutive forms of the everlasting flowers sold by florists and, indeed, belong to the same family. As their name suggests, these too can be preserved by drying.

When plants are seen grouped, as in the habitat photograph of male plants, it is easy to understand why the mountain everlasting is sometimes referred to as the Scottish edelweiss.

[the blue flowers growing with the mountain everlasting are heath milkwort.]

Close up of a male flower head

The seemingly wiry stems, which in this location usually grow to no more than 15 cm, are initially bent almost double before straightening quite rapidly to reveal the flowers.

27

Heath Milkwort

[milkwort family]

As its name infers, it is found in heath-like (acidic) areas of the meadow. It has a scrambling growth habit and the tiny flowers, in this locality vary from quite intense blue to light blue, with shades of pink. There are various suggestions concerning the origin of the name 'milkwort'. One is that milk production is increased in cattle that graze where it is plentiful.

The flowers certainly deserve a closer look with a magnifying glass. I have always considered, perhaps fancifully, that they resemble miniature orchids.

Petty Whin

[pea family]

Petty whin is found on only a limited number of drier sites on the slope of a knoll. It can perhaps be best likened to a miniature gorse, but is always low growing. The yellow flowers form on rather wiry stems with not very conspicuous spines which are nothing like as 'fierce' as those on gorse.

Lousewort

[figwort family]

Lousewort is found in the wetter, acidic but not too boggy areas of the meadow. Its generic scientific name *Pedicularis* is derived from the Latin *pedis*, for louse. and its common name indicates that it was believed to transmit lice to sheep. It is, in fact, a hemiparasite, the first that we have encountered. Such plants, on the meadow, attach themselves to the roots of grasses and take water and mineral salts from their hosts. They are called hemiparasites because they photosynthesise in the normal way and do not, therefore, take sugars from their hosts and so satisfy their own energy requirements.

Bugle

[dead-nettle family]

This is found widely on the meadow, usually where the grass is damp and the soil heavy. The erect stems, of no more than 15 cm, have blue flowers over at least half their height.

The flowering stems arise from low creeping stems that root readily when in contact with the ground. As can be seen from the photograph, this feature enables bugle to spread widely. Horticultural varieties are commonly sold as plants for 'ground cover'.

Bilberry

[heather family]

Bilberry is found in the poorer, more acid soils of the meadow. The fruit is renowned for its flavour. Beside the many ways it can be consumed by humans, it is also eaten by grouse and other birds. The pendulous flowers produce abundant nectar and are visited by a range of insects. The small leaves are seasonal, appearing in the spring and falling off in the autumn. However, the stems remain green throughout the year and enable the plant to photosynthesise when conditions are favourable in early spring, before the leaves are formed, and so get a good start. Bilberry is also found in woodlands, especially where the tree canopy is fairly open. So this is another example of a plant that may indicate the presence of trees in the area at one time.

32

Bog-myrtle

[bog-myrtle family]

The first time that I came across this plant I thought it was a patch of a rather nondescript willow shrub about one metre in height. A year or so later, when passing the same plants before any leaves had appeared, my eyes were drawn to the colour created by numerous catkins, but these were not the catkins of a willow.

Male catkins (about 10 mm in length)

As with willow, however, there are both male and female catkins, and these usually occur on different plants. Remarkably however, the plant can change sex! If, say, a plant produces male catkins one year it might produce female the next, and vice versa.

Bog-myrtle lives up to its name, being found in distinctly boggy areas. The surface of the leaves and stems are covered in resin glands (white spots in the photographs) which produce an aromatic oil that gives off a distinctive pleasant odour when the plant is crushed. This feature gives rise to the alternative name of sweet gale. Twigs of the plant have traditionally been used to deter the Scottish midge as well as other biting insects.

Female catkin (about 5 mm in length)

Mountain Pansy

[violet family]

One of the highlights of the grassy areas of the meadow has to be the mountain pansies. As their name suggests, they are typically upland plants and are usually associated with a base-rich soil. They have a long flowering season and whilst they are readily seen in May and early June, when grasses are still low, flowers can be found well into August.

The scientific name for mountain pansy is *Viola lutea*

[Latin *lutea* = yellow]

The flower stems of mountain pansy arise from rhizomes or underground creeping stems. These persist from year to year making this pansy a perennial plant, in contrast to the more common wild pansy, which is an annual growing anew from seed each year.

In addition to yellow flowers there are also bluish purple and many variations between.

I have always found it both surprising and interesting that so many colour variations can be found within a relatively small area. The flower heads shown on the previous page were all photographed on plants within a radius of about 500m from a place where the car was commonly parked.

Pansies are especially eye catching when they occur in small patches, all of the same colour, brought about by the spread of an original 'parent' plant by means of rhizomes.

Whilst non-flowering plants such as mosses and ferns may not immediately attract the same attention as those producing flowers, they do nevertheless provide a welcome addition to the breadth of the Plant Kingdom represented on the meadow.

Polytrichum juniperum

It is easy to overlook or dismiss mosses as uninteresting. I would venture to suggest, however, that the male plants of this moss, with their geometrically arranged and brightly coloured leaves bearing microscopic reproductive structures, are worth a closer look. They are sometimes, incorrectly, referred to as moss 'flowers'.

Field Horsetail

During May the brown fertile stems of this fern appear, bearing cone-like structures within which large numbers of spores are produced. The energy and materials required to form these fertile stems come from stores in other stems, underground, called rhizomes. Later, the vegetative (non-fertile stems) appear with whorls of green photosynthetic branches. It is the form of these that gives rise to the common name.

Male Fern

The preferred habitat of this fern is quite definitely the base of drystane dykes. The unfurling of the robust fronds, with their attractive crosier-like appearance, is another welcome indication that spring is well on the way.

At one time Fungi were classified with non-flowering plants. It has become apparent, however, that Fungi are a distinct entity and as a result have been given a separate Kingdom.

Morel

Whilst autumn is the time of year most associated with the appearance of toadstools (more properly, the fruiting bodies of fungi) the morel, with its distinctive cap of ridges and surface depressions on which spores are produced, is a spring species.

In springtime many of the animals can readily draw your attention for one reason or another

Curlew

During April the meadow echoes to the evocative bubbling call of the first of the returning wading birds*, the curlew. The photograph of this pair was taken one early evening when a stiff, cool breeze was blowing – they seemed to be just 'sitting it out'! Soon they will be claiming a nest site, often in some of the damper grassy areas.

[*The term wader is applied to birds which, typically, have both long legs and long beaks in relation to the size of their bodies. This arrangement allows them to wade out on to mud flats, and also wet areas of marshland, to feed during the winter months. In the spring they return to meadows and moorlands to nest.]

Buzzard

The 'mewing' call of buzzards is, like that of the curlew, another evocative sound heard as they float apparently effortlessly over the grassland, looking for prey such as rabbits or hares.

Mistle Thrush

Another 'early bird' is the mistle thrush. This, the largest of the British thrushes, is present throughout the year. The brown spots on the breast are bigger and more widely spaced than those of the song thrush, and it has an overall greyer appearance, especially noticeable when it flies. Mistle thrushes nest in the conifer plantations, from which they make quite short sorties to adjacent grassland to collect worms and insects. Males often sing from tops of the conifers. They are good mimics and in this locality are not unknown to capture the 'mewing' call of the buzzard to perfection!

Common (Grey) Partridge

The common or grey partridge, in spite of its name, is seen relatively rarely on the meadow. The female should be about to lay her eggs. The male can be distinguished from the female by the slightly brighter colours on head and neck, as well as the dark inverted U on its front.

A pair

Male bird

Greylag Goose

Greylag geese are present on one of the local lochs and on occasions they visit the meadow. Often they do so in the early morning, which is when this photograph was taken. In contrast to greylags found in parks, where they are used to being fed and are 'tame', these birds are wild and very wary. I took this photograph using a telephoto lens and was some distance away, but they were well aware of my presence. Their 'honking' flight calls are very similar to those of farmyard geese, to which are distantly related.

Mountain (Blue) Hare

Signs of the changing season can also be seen in the appearance of the mountain (or blue) hare. The thick white winter coat is being shed to reveal its brown summer coat, which is shorter and less dense. With the absence of snow they are readily visible whilst this shedding is occurring. In spite of their scientific name *Lepus timidus*, mountain hares can be quite inquisitive when approached carefully, indeed, if you remain still they may well approach to 'check you out'. In the case of this particular hare, it took a good look at me in response to my steady approach, but once I stopped and I remained still it went on feeding.

The upper (higher) area of the meadow seems to be about as low down as mountain hares come from the nearby mountains, and this part of their range overlaps with that of the brown hares.

Roe Deer

Roe deer are quite numerous mammals on the meadow. Whilst they are most likely to be seen at dawn and dusk, they can often be found grazing in quiet areas during the daytime. Over winter they have a thick dark coloured coat, which in some animals can be almost black.

The antlers of the buck are shed late in the year and new ones grow during the early months of the following year. The new antlers are first covered in velvet* and towards the end of April a buck will brash his antlers against a tree to remove this.

[*Velvet is a well vascularised 'skin' that covers the antlers and supplies the materials for their growth. When fully developed, the blood supply to the velvet is 'switched off' and it withers, at which stage the deer brashes it off.]

Roe buck with freshly cleaned antlers, which are still partly blood stained.

Also, by this stage of the year, does are nearing the time when their young (commonly twins) will be born.

Mid Summer
(June)

As May merges into June we are only three weeks away from mid-summer. With the long daylight hours in the Scottish Highlands, the rate of plant growth increases (especially the grasses), as does the number of species in flower. Also, animal activity reaches a peak.

A feature which, to my eyes, epitomises this transition is the leafing out of the trees and bushes into their resplendent fresh green colours.

Downy Birch

[birch family]

There are many downy birch trees on the meadow, mostly occurring in stands. This lone tree is a particularly fine specimen, enhanced by the backdrop of the mountains.

[Note that there is still a pocket of snow on one of the distant mountains.]

Beech

[beech family]

There are a number of beech trees on the meadow and, like the lone birch, this is a fine specimen. In the autumn the fruit containing seeds ('mast') form a valuable food source for various animals, including squirrels and tits.

49

Wild Cherry

[rose family]

This wild cherry, widely known as 'gean' in Scotland, is a one-off on the meadow. The original tree, which must have been some size and age, seems to have fallen down a long time ago. However, somehow it has managed to produce substantial new branches which produce blossom with unfailing regularity every June. The scientific name for the wild cherry is *Prunus avium*. The species name is derived from the Latin word *avis* for a bird. Certainly, for some reason, the cherries disappear very quickly!

Northern Marsh-orchid

[orchid family]

The appearance of the northern marsh-orchid is a harbinger of the orchid show to come. The colour of the flowers always reminds me of the food colouring dye cochineal and this certainly makes them stand out.

Chickweed-wintergreen

[primrose family]

Chickweed-wintergreen, with its dainty white flowers, may be found both on open ground in drier acid areas, as well as in mossy places in the shade of birch trees. When present on open ground it is often mixed in with a species of *Cladonia* lichen, as seen in this photograph.

Kidney Vetch

[pea family]

The sprawling flowers of the kidney vetch only seem to last for a short time. This plant prefers drier, well drained grassy areas and its presence suggests that the soil on which it is growing is base-rich.

Fairy Flax

[flax family]

The tiny white flowers seen with the kidney vetch are those of fairy flax. The two species are frequently found growing together, since fairy flax is another plant that prefers a base-rich soil.

53

Lady's-mantle

[rose family]

Whilst not particularly conspicuous, lady's-mantle, with its distinctive, partially lobed leaves, may be found in grassy areas.

Brooklime

[figwort family]

Throughout the meadow there are numerous small, muddy drainage ditches. Brooklime frequents the edges of such ditches and its stems grow out over the water, taking root in the process. The deep blue flowers are borne on flower stalks that protrude from the stem, which enhances their visibility in spite of their small size.

Common Bird's-foot-trefoil

[pea family]

In contrast to lady's mantle, the common bird's-foot-trefoil is a showy plant that sometimes occurs in quite large patches. The habitat photograph shows such a patch completely covering a hidden tree stump. Each patch is formed from a single original plant. This puts down a tap root and then produces horizontal stems (stolons) which branch out and root as they grow, a strategy that allows successful recovery from grazing. Flowering stems arise from wherever the horizontal stems take root.

The buds are often marked with red before they open.

Common bird's-foot-trefoil is usually found in drier areas of the grassland and on drystane dykes. It is another plant that is commonly, but not exclusively, associated with base-rich soils.

This photograph was taken at the end of June and the yellow flowers of common bird's-foot-trefoil contrast pleasantly with the pink/purple flowers of emerging wild thyme.

Marsh Cinquefoil

[rose family]

The cinquefoils are plants which derive their name from the fact that the leaves comprise five leaflets. The marsh cinquefoil inhabits damp marshy areas and its flowers have sepals that are longer than the petals. Both are coloured a distinctive purple-red.

Common Rock-rose

[rock-rose family]

The common rock-rose, with its sulphur coloured flowers, is usually an indication that the associated soil is base-rich. It is found in drier areas where the vegetation is short and, living up to its name, often grows at the base of drystane dykes or in pockets of soil higher up. The flowers, seen at their best when the sun is out, do not last very long, seeming to shed their petals quite readily. The formal name for the plant, *Helianthemum nummularium*, is derived from the Latin meaning 'sunflower'.

Heath Spotted-orchid

[orchid family]

The heath spotted-orchid is the commonest of the orchids and, as its name suggests, prefers heath-like acidic soils. Numbers may vary from just a few plants at a particular location to, in some instances, great swathes.

The colour of the heath spotted-orchid flowers may vary from almost white, tinged with pink, through light pink to deep purplish pink. The flower colour of the left hand specimen is particularly deep. This raises the possibility that it may be a hybrid cross between a heath spotted-orchid and a northern marsh-orchid. Hybridization between orchids of different species is a frequent occurrence. However, ascertaining that an orchid is a hybrid is fraught with difficulty, often requiring genetic analysis.

Alpine Bistort

[knotweed family]

A habitat photograph showing the typical random distribution of this species. [The yellow flowers in the foreground are rock rose.]

Alpine bistort is a plant associated with mountain grasslands. The flowering spike is quite distinctive, having closely packed whiteish flowers on the upper part of the spike and small reddish brown bulbils on the lower section. This arrangement is a dual strategy to ensure propagation. Assuming insects visit the flowers, then pollination will lead to the production of seed. The bulbils, on the other hand, are vegetative (asexual) structures and do not need pollination by insects for their production. When ripe they usually drop to the ground and grow into new plants that are genetically identical to the parent plant. At this elevation insects are usually in good supply, regardless of the quality of the season, but this may not be the case in grasslands at higher altitudes. In such circumstances the strategy will pay off. Indeed the ratio of bulbils to flowers increases with gain in altitude.

Occasionally the bulbils start to develop whilst on the spike, which gives the plant a very odd appearance.

63

Wood Crane's-bill

[crane's-bill family]

The wood crane's-bill, a relative of the garden geranium, is sparsely scattered and may be found both in the dappled shade of birch trees as well as in open grassy areas. The flowers are a distinctive bluish-purple.

Creeping Willow

[willow family]

We have already met this plant as a harbinger of spring, noting that then it was only the diminutive male catkins that might draw one's attention. In contrast, however, the female seeding catkins which occur in summer are highly visible, having the appearance of being covered in cotton wool. It has been suggested that the fibres act rather like a fleece, making the internal temperature higher than the surrounding air; if so this would aid the development of the seeds.

Scottish Asphodel

[lily family]

This is another small plant of base-rich higher ground that is easily overlooked. It was growing in a damp area near the willow. I am not sure I would have spotted it if it had not been close to the willow, which had drawn my attention. The flattened leaves, a distinctive feature, arise from a basal tuft and resemble, in miniature, those of an iris. In this photograph most of the leaves are hidden by the vegetation, but a few are visible in the centre of the bottom edge.

Purple Milk-vetch

[pea family]

The purple milk-vetch is another indicator of base-rich soils. The flower heads are dense clusters of purple/mauve-coloured, pea-like flowers borne on stems above the level of the leaves. They are usually found where the grasses are short, and plants often occur in closely knit groups which makes them distinctly eye catching.

Meadow Buttercup

[buttercup family]

The meadow buttercup is always present as one of the grassland plants and in some years may flourish to provide a spectacular carpet of yellow, as here. For some seemingly obscure reason, it remains relatively inconspicuous in other years. The yellow colour of butter was, in folk law, believed to be caused by cattle eating buttercups, hence the vernacular name. However buttercups contain a bitter tasting oil and cattle avoid eating them. The scientific name *Ranunculus acris* reflects this; the Latin *acris* translates as sharp or bitter tasting.

Cuckooflower

[cabbage family]

The cuckoo returns at this time of year, making its presence known, even if it is rarely seen, for the call of the male birds carries some distance from where it is perched, often in a tall conifer. The cuckooflower takes its common name from the fact that its flowering period coincides with the arrival of the cuckoo. Plants are found in damper areas of the grassland, where their lilac flowers add a splash of colour.

Bog Pondweed

[pondweed family]

This is perhaps a rather prosaic plant at first sight, found growing in boggy ground or in shallow, sometimes slow moving, water. Examining a photomicrograph of a cross-section of the internal structure of the stem, however, reveals an interesting architecture.

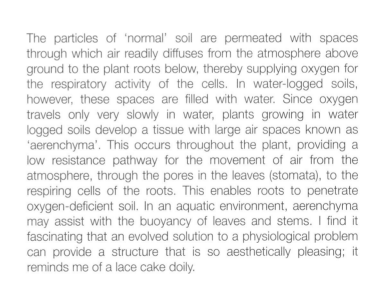

The particles of 'normal' soil are permeated with spaces through which air readily diffuses from the atmosphere above ground to the plant roots below, thereby supplying oxygen for the respiratory activity of the cells. In water-logged soils, however, these spaces are filled with water. Since oxygen travels only very slowly in water, plants growing in water logged soils develop a tissue with large air spaces known as 'aerenchyma'. This occurs throughout the plant, providing a low resistance pathway for the movement of air from the atmosphere, through the pores in the leaves (stomata), to the respiring cells of the roots. This enables roots to penetrate oxygen-deficient soil. In an aquatic environment, aerenchyma may assist with the buoyancy of leaves and stems. I find it fascinating that an evolved solution to a physiological problem can provide a structure that is so aesthetically pleasing; it reminds me of a lace cake doily.

Marsh-marigold

[buttercup family]

The marsh-marigold is a showy member of the buttercup family, unlike the true marigold, which is a member of the daisy family. The rich yellow flowers of the marsh-marigold, often as wide as 5 cm in diameter, are held firmly aloft on stout stems.

The plants are found on wetter parts of the grassland, quite commonly growing in and revealing otherwise invisible channels through which water slowly percolates.

Bogbean

[bogbean family]

The name bogbean sounds dull, but the plant itself is fascinating. Whilst it often does grow in bogs, it may also be found rooted in the relatively shallow margins of lochs, as here. From this position it produces thick stems that spread out for a considerable distance just under the surface of the water, held there by the large air spaces which provide buoyancy. The trifoliate leaves, which are attractive in their own right, are held above the water on long stems. It is the flowers, however, that make this plant special. These occur in spikes, also held well above the water, and the individual flowers are white inside progressing to pink at the outside where they are fringed with white hairs. It is a great pity that the period during which these beautiful flowers may be seen is relatively short.

In early spring I have sometimes seen roe deer, in the shallow margins of the loch, pulling the floating bogbean stems out of the water and then grazing them.

Common Butterwort

[bladderwort family]

The common butterwort is one of two insectivorous plants found on the meadow. The flowers are pinkish blue and the leaves a distinctive yellowish green. The leaf surfaces look waxy and the longitudinal margins are rolled inwards. The upper surface is covered with large numbers of minute glands on short stalks. Each secretes a globule of sticky mucilage and it is this that creates the impression of waxiness. Insects landing on a leaf are caught in the mucilage and as they struggle encounter more and more of the sticky globules. Along with the many stalked glands there is also a greater number of smaller, stalk-less glands which, when an insect is caught, produce digestive enzymes. These dissolve all but the outer parts (exoskeleton) of the insect releasing nutrients that are absorbed through the leaf surface. Whilst the colour of the leaves, which are arranged in a rosette, make the plant very visible to humans, it is something of a mystery what actually make them attractive to insects.

Examination of a leaf will usually reveal a large number of small (midge sized) insects trapped on the surface. Many people state that the leaves actively curl inwards to digest the prey and then uncurl when digestion is complete. This may occur if a large insect is trapped, but for the most part, once a leaf has opened it seems to remain open and small insects are simply trapped passively. However, rolled longitudinal edges of a leaf do make it difficult for small insects to escape the surface, even if there is no active curling.

Common butterwort is so called because the leaves of the plant may be used to coagulate milk in the manufacture of butter - a sort of vegetable rennet. This is due to bacteria in the mucilage (not the enzymes).

An alternative name for common butterwort is 'bog violet'. This seems quite apt looking at the flowers.

72

The preferred habitat of common butterwort is damp soils or crevices in wet rock surfaces. Whilst most insectivorous plants are found in acid conditions, common butterwort is unusual in that it can be found on soils ranging from acid to alkaline. However, the wet conditions in which it grows would suggest reduced activity of the soil bacteria that recycle plant nutrients, in common with the situation in the acid conditions in which the majority of insectivorous plants are found.

Globeflower

[buttercup family]

The aptly named globeflower is a splendid plant found in damper areas of the grassland. Whilst always present, rather like the meadow buttercup, in some years it provides a magnificent display, as shown in the habitat photograph.

The 'globe' is formed from stiff overlapping sepals, the petals being smaller and hidden within the globe. The transfer of pollen between flower heads is known to be effected by small flies that are able to squeeze between the stiff sepals. However, on occasions I have observed bumblebees forcing their way into a flower, the sepals making a distinct crackling sound in the process.

Stag's-horn Clubmoss

Another plant easily overlooked is the stag's-horn clubmoss, a species more closely related to ferns and horsetails than the true mosses. The twin cones which produce the spores of this primitive plant give it its common name. When these are absent the ground-hugging, branching stems, closely covered with small leaves, may easily be mistaken for a true moss. There are, however, significant differences. For example, vascular tissues comprising xylem and phloem, which transport water and sugars to and from the leaves respectively, are present in flowering plants, conifers, ferns and clubmosses. It is the vascular tissues in the stems of the clubmoss that provide the springy or wiry feel when touched. However, such tissues are not found in mosses, which at the best possess only primitive water- and sugar-conducting tissues. Another difference is that the stems of clubmosses bear roots, which anchor the plant in the soil, extracting from it both minerals and water. Mosses, on the other hand, lack these characteristic features of most land plants, possessing only hair-like rhizoids which anchor them to the ground but have no significant absorptive function.

Polypody

The fronds of the fern polypody, bearing leaflets bluntly rounded at their tips, are produced from creeping 'stems'. These grow in a variety of directions, hence the name 'many footed'. On the meadow it adds to the character of drystane dykes.

Maidenhair Spleenwort

The maidenhair spleenwort is an attractive fern that grows in crevices on drystane dykes. The leaflets are supported on distinctive, thin black wiry 'stems'. Together the fronds have an almost rosette-like appearance. The term 'maidenhair' suggests that the fronds bear some resemblance to the maidenhair fern. The latter is commonly cultivated and sold in shops, but is rare in the wild and belongs to an entirely different genus from the spleenwort.

Moonwort Fern

The moonwort fern is found in some of the drier, grassy areas. It has unusual leaflets which, by stretching the imagination a little, may be thought of as 'half moons'. Having spotted something so distinctive, one might wonder why it had not been seen before, but moonwort plants are remarkably easy to overlook. This specimen caught my attention as it was illuminated by the final rays of evening sunlight.

Towards the end of May and during June many animals are visibly involved in producing and raising offspring.

Common Buzzard

Buzzards usually nest in trees and around the meadow take advantage of the conifer plantations, where they can be seen displaying near the nest site.

Curlew

The relative peace of the meadow is periodically shattered by numbers of these birds taking to the air, almost simultaneously, from various points. This may be in response to a threat, such as a bird of prey flying over, but frequently there is no immediately apparent cause. The vocal out-pouring usually soon ceases as abruptly as it started.

80

Curlews will just as readily call whilst on the ground as in the air.

Curlew eggs usually start hatching towards the end of May but this can extend into June. It is during this time that the parents are most vocal, with their characteristic warning calls to their offspring carrying considerable distances.

The young are active well into June and sometimes the beginning of July. However, a 'parent' is not above trying to get 'forty winks' as 'junior' heads off to explore! It would seem that parenting is restricted to warning the young of potential danger, and apart from that they seem to be left very much to their own devices to find food.

Lapwing

The lapwing is another wading bird which nests in places where the grass is fairly short. It is also known as the green plover, a reference to the green tinge to its wing feathers and the fact that it is a member of the plover family. It also has a third, commonly used onomatopoeic name, the 'peewit', which mimics the characteristic call as it performs an aerial twisting flight over the nesting territory. Rather like curlews, lapwings soon leave the young to find their own food, but if danger threatens, as when a buzzard flies overhead, they run to a parent and hide under its wings.

Redshank

The redshank is a wader that is seen only very occasionally on the meadow. The bird is in its summer breeding plumage, which is more strongly marked than in winter. The name derives from the long, orange-red legs that are highly visible in flight or when wintering on mud flats, but are less so in grass. I have never seen either display or young; it is probable that nesting occurs in marshy grassland adjacent to a nearby loch.

Oystercatcher

The oystercatcher is a very dapper wader with its sharply divided black and white plumage and thick orange coloured bill. At times single birds, or groups of them, appear on the top of a drystane dyke and their 'piping' generates a lot of noise. When paired they display by strutting along almost side by side, piping again as they do so. The female usually nests in a natural depression in the grassland and, in spite of her size and the fact that she is anything but camouflaged, she may be remarkably difficult to spot as she simple ducks her head when anything approaches. The male, meanwhile, will often fly about, patrolling in the vicinity of the nest.

The young follow their parents about for quite a while before becoming independent.

Whilst most waders effectively allow their young to fend for themselves regarding feeding, my own observations of oystercatchers, over a number of years, indicate that the parent birds do provide some level of supervision.

Carrion Crow

One bird that is present throughout the year, nesting in the local trees, is the carrion crow. At times quite large numbers are present and this is not good news for ground nesting birds as they are predators of both eggs and young, coming down to the area of a nest when alerted to its position by a bird flying away. I remember one particular occasion, however, when two crows alighted close to the nest of a lapwing and although they quartered the ground for a long time whilst the parents dive bombed them, they nevertheless failed to locate the nest and the eggs. This would seem to demonstrate the advantage of the cryptic camouflage of lapwing eggs, a characteristic shared with many ground nesting birds. As their name suggests, carrion crows do feed on carrion such as dead sheep or lambs, but have a bad reputation for not being above attacking live sheep and especially lambs.

Wren

This wren made its presence known with its repeated sharp 'tic-tic-tic' call when I was on the way to photograph a particular plant. I was rather taken by surprise; as wren is an uncommon bird on the meadow. As usual I was carrying my second camera set up with a medium telephoto lens 'just in case', which allowed me to take a shot before moving away. Just as I was starting to move I suddenly saw the youngster, level with my elbow, lying absolutely doggo, and could not resist a shot as I retreated

Coal Tit

Coal tits are readily distinguishable by the small white patch on the back of their heads (though this is not visible in this photograph). They are numerous in the conifer plantations, displaying considerable acrobatic skills when searching for insects. Coal tits most commonly nest in holes in trees but, as can be seen in the photograph, will also use crevices in a drystane dyke.

Pied Wagtail

One bird that often advertises its presence with its buoyant flight, calling as it does so, is the pied wagtail. This is another bird that nests in holes and crevices that can conveniently be found in drystane dykes. In one part of the meadow, where a narrow road runs alongside a wall, they may often be seen searching for flies and other insects (their main diet) resting on the surface of the road; in this case in the warmth of the late evening.

A juvenile

89

Rabbit

In some years rabbits may be present in almost plague proportions. These animals may look cute, but from a practical point of view there can be no doubt that large numbers significantly reduce the grass potentially available for cattle and sheep. They often graze the grass down to a level at which growth recovery is severely impaired, an effect that can be clearly seen in the photograph of the warren. Undoubtedly the greatest influence on the rabbit population over the years that I have visited the meadow is myxamytosis. Whilst this disease is probably present at some level all the time in rabbit populations, every so often it makes an obvious reappearance. Sometime after the photograph was taken the disease took a hold again and two years later grasses in the area were well above knee height and I managed to twist my ankle in a hidden entrance to a burrow!

Hares

By this time in the year it is not so easy to distinguish the brown hare from the mountain hare as both have brown fur. When comparing the two, however, the mountain hare can be distinguished by its shorter ears, longer hind feet and the absence of black on the tail (see the photograph of one running). The brown hare, in contrast, has a black mark on the upper part of its tail, clearly visible as it runs away. Also, having lost its white fur, the mouth and nose of a mountain hare can look slightly 'pinched' when compared to the brown. From a distance the blue hare can be seen to have a more bouncing gait than that of the brown, especially when running over longish vegetation.

Both hares can adopt a low profile when resting, as demonstrated by this brown hare. In this situation the position of the eyes close to the top of the head provides good visibility.

During the breeding season skirmishes between brown hares are well known but it is less widely appreciated that mountain hares also indulge in this behaviour. The two brown in the photograph were shaping up for such an encounter but vanished when a hill walker with a dog appeared.

Roe Deer

By this time in the year the roe deer are shedding their dark winter coats, a process that gives them a rather scruffy appearance for a while.

However this soon reveals a rather smart looking, reddish summer coat.

The best time to see roe deer is either early or late in the day, although they may also be seen during the middle of the day in quieter secluded areas. After feeding they will lie up for what can be quite a long time whilst ruminating. It is remarkable how adept they are at making themselves 'invisible' during this process, even in short vegetation. This is well illustrated by the two in the photograph. Something has attracted the attention of the doe but the buck* is still keeping a low profile, as can be seen more clearly in the enlarged view.

[*The buck is still in velvet which indicates that probably it is in its first year. It is quite usual for them to shed their velvet later than mature animals.]

93

It is always a welcome sight to see the first butterflies in June. Two that consistently lead the way in ushering in the butterfly season are the small pearl-bordered fritillary and the orange tip.

Small Pearl-bordered Fritillary

This is a species of butterfly that I have found very frustrating to try to photograph. Whilst they commonly remain in visual contact they fly quickly low over the ground, occasionally alighting briefly on a flower to refuel with nectar. I have experienced a high failure rate with a butterfly moving on before I have managed to position myself and focus, never mind press the shutter! The food plant of the caterpillar is the dog violet, eggs being laid on the undersurface of leaves or stems, although they may sometimes be dropped near the plant.

Orange Tip

It is the distinctive bright orange tips of the forewings of the male that give this species its name. Those of the female, in contrast, are almost black, making it quite easy to mistake it for other species of 'white' butterflies. On the meadow the orange tip is associated with cuckooflower plants. Eggs are laid on these plants and orange tip caterpillars feed on the flowers and seed pods.

High Summer
(July)

By the beginning of July, in areas where grasses are present, these often dominate many of the other flowering plants that grow amongst them. This is also the month when one becomes particularly aware of insects; on sunny days there is always a background buzz, punctuated by the chirping of grasshoppers. Butterflies and some other insects draw one's attention visually, whilst in the evenings midges invariably make their presence known!

Dog-rose

[rose family]

The dog-rose flowers as June progresses into July. It is not a widespread plant, but the vicious hooked thorns seem to protect it from the attention of grazing animals. The showy flowers attract a variety of insects that collect pollen from the numerous stamens; though no nectar is produced.

97

Wild Strawberry

[rose family]

The wild strawberry resembles a miniature garden strawberry. This member of the rose family has flowered during June and is already producing the 'berries'. Like the garden plant it produces new plants from runners which are red in colour; one is visible in the photograph towards the left hand side of the bottom edge. The wild strawberry is commonly, but not exclusively, associated with base-rich soils.

Selfheal

[dead-nettle family]

Selfheal is well known as a common invasive weed of lawns, spreading by creeping stems. In a natural environment, it is typically found growing amongst grasses that are short or on bare patches of ground, where it will grow up to 30 cm. Violet coloured flowers are common amongst members of the dead-nettle family but, unlike most mints, selfheal lacks any aromatic odour when its leaves are handled.

Meadow Vetchling

[pea family]

The meadow vetchling, like the birds-foot trefoil, is a member of the pea family with yellow flowers. It displays a different growth form, however, as its rather weak stem scrambles upwards, gaining support from the surrounding vegetation with the aid of small tendrils, produced at the ends of modified leaves. Being a member of the pea family, meadow vetchling always produces root nodules which fix atmospheric nitrogen into nitrogenous salts.

Tufted Vetch

[pea family]

The numerous flowers on the heads of tufted vetch make it a very visible plant, whether it is spread out over an area where there is insufficient vegetation to provide suitable support, or climbing through grasses with the aid of its tendrils. The flowers are a bluish purple/violet, a colour which seems to vary depending on whether the sun is shining or not.

White and Red Clover

[pea family]

The clovers, like the other members of the pea family, possess nitrogen-fixing root nodules. The white clover seems to hug the ground, spreading by means of creeping stems that root as they grow. As a result it forms extensive, close-knit patches, almost to the exclusion of other vegetation. Curiously, though, a large patch that has grown vigorously for a year or two may simply disappear for no apparent reason.

Plants of red clover are more diffuse than those of white clover and seem to mix in well with other vegetation. The location of this species is much more predictable from year to another.

Not only do clovers enrich the soil with nitrogen, but the flowers produce a good supply of nectar at the bottom of the flower tubes. Bees, especially bumble bees, make good use of this rich food source.

Oxeye Daisy

[daisy family]

The oxeye daisy, the largest of our native daisies, seems to demand attention wherever it grows. The large white and yellow flower heads are borne singly on tall stems arising from a rosette of basal leaves. The scientific name now adopted for the daisy family is Asteraceae. Formerly it was Compositae, which made the point that this plant has a 'composite flower', like all members of the daisy family, the flower head being made up of a large number of small, individual flowers (florets) supported on the flattened end of the flower stalk – the receptacle. Each floret in the outermost ring has a large white 'strap' and is known as a ray floret whilst the golden yellow disc florets of the central area look like small tubes.

Daisy

[Asteraceae]

This particular daisy plant was growing on a drystane dyke. I found it interesting to see this ubiquitous species expressing its full potential rather than being cut down to size in a lawn as is commonly the situation. The scientific name for the daisy is *Bellis perennis* and the generic name *bellis* is derived from the Latin meaning 'pretty, handsome or beautiful'.

Bog Asphodel

[lily family]

As its name suggests, bog asphodel is found growing on bogs and other wet acidic soils.

Despite being an attractive plant, its specific scientific name, [*Narthecium*] *ossifragum*, is derived from two Latin words meaning 'bone' and 'breaker'. The reason is that shepherds blamed this plant for the brittleness of bones in sheep which had eaten it. As the plant grows in soils low in nutrients, however, this is the more likely cause of the problem.

Bog asphodel has creeping roots and, as can be seen from the habitat photograph, these enable it to spread and form what can be quite extensive patches.

The flowering stems are up to 50 cm high, and a spike of the yellow to orange flowers is most certainly worth a closer look. The individual flowers are like miniature lilies and are simply exquisite with their yellow petals and sepals encircling the woolly yellow stamens tipped with orange.

Common Wintergreen

[wintergreen family]

The 'lily of the valley' of the meadow (though not related) is a small plant, some 18 cm high. The drooping 'globe like' flowers are white shot with pink and make an unusual, though not particularly visible, addition to the flora. Despite its name common wintergreen is not very abundant, being found only in a few sites that are for the most part both damp and shady. The flowers apparently do not produce nectar and pollination is mostly likely effected by visits from beetles.

Meadowsweet

[rose family]

This is another plant that inhabits damp sites. As can be seen from the photograph, it is capable of covering an extensive area. When seen 'en masse' the tightly packed clusters of small flowers at the ends of tall and robust stems give the impression of a sea of foam, from which arises a pleasant if rather overpowering fragrance.

109

Ragged-Robin

[pink family]

During July some of the wetter areas of the meadow are a haze of pink with the flowers of ragged-robin, as the above and the previous habitat photographs illustrate. It is well named, for the flowers do indeed look ragged with their deeply incised petals. They seem to be popular with green-veined butterflies, which probably assist with pollination.

Occasional white flowers may occur sometimes amongst the pink ones, although close examination invariably reveals a hint of pink.

Water Forget-me-not

[borage family]

The water forget-me-not, with its distinctive light blue flowers and yellow 'eyes', seems very much at home on the river margin.

The large green leaves are of colt's-foot, having appeared after the flowers died back in spring.

Common Sorrel

[knotweed family]

I have always considered sorrels, and for that matter docks, to be rather mundane plants that are nuisance weeds in the garden. In this context, however, I was differently persuaded; somehow these plants add a dash of colour to the surroundings.

Purple Moor-grass

[grass family]

This is a grass of wet acidic sites and its characteristic, long purple flowering spikes grow from tight clumps, adding a bit of character to what are often rather bland surroundings.

Yorkshire-fog

[grass family]

Yorkshire-fog is a coarse grass unwelcome in lawns. Yet when seen growing to its full height and flowering in clumps like this, it is not unattractive and it certainly stands out from the surrounding vegetation. I think of this as the 'pampas grass' of the meadow. Since it seems to survive the attention of grazing animals, it is presumably not particularly palatable.

Cottongrass

[sedge family]

Cottongrasses are found in marshy or boggy areas. The name is misleading, for these are sedges rather than true grasses. Their flowers, though they may not immediately draw one's attention, are nevertheless most attractive when seen close up. Their presence becomes highly visible, however, during the production of seeds: white bristles, associated with the ovary wall, elongate considerably to eventually embrace the whole ovary containing the developing seeds with what looks like 'cotton wool'. As is the case with the seeding creeping willow, it is possible that this cotton wool cocoon may trap solar radiation, a greenhouse effect in miniature, and so provide more favourable conditions for the process of seed production.

Germander Speedwell

[figwort family]

The stems of this sprawling speedwell root at frequent intervals and at these points produce upward projecting stems bearing masses of small, brilliant sky blue flowers which make this otherwise inconspicuous plant stand out amongst the surrounding grasses.

Red Bartsia

[figwort family]

Red bartsia is a short rather inconspicuous plant which grows amongst grasses and is a hemiparasite on them.

Marsh Lousewort

[figwort family]

In contrast to the low growing, compact lousewort, the flowers of the marsh lousewort are borne on vertical stems. Whilst the flowers of the two species are superficially similar, those of the marsh lousewort are a distinctly deeper colour and tend towards red rather than pink. An alternative common name for this plant is 'red-rattle', arising from the fact that if the mature dry fruiting structures are shaken, the loose seeds rattle against the dry walls. Like lousewort, marsh lousewort is a hemiparasite.

Yellow-rattle

[figwort family]

Yellow-rattle is another short, hemiparasitic plant growing amongst grasses, although it is more easily spotted than red bartsia, with which it is commonly associated. The common name derives from the fact that, like marsh lousewort (red-rattle), the seeds rattle within the fruiting structures as these mature and dry out.

Yellow-rattle, along with many hemiparasites in grassland, by taking water and minerals from grasses reduces their vigour. As a consequence they are less able to dominate flowering herbaceous plants in competing for resources, including light. This fosters plant diversity. For this reason yellow-rattle is widely used by conservationists when attempting to increase the number of plant species in grassland that has, for one reason or another, become species poor. At first sight it might seem that reducing the vigour of grasses would be to the detriment of grassland associated with livestock production. However, nature is never so simple. Evidence is now emerging that yellow-rattle, and possibly other hemiparasites of grassland, may have beneficial effects on soil fertility by, for example, increasing the rate at which nitrogen is recycled.

Heath Speedwell

[figwort family]

This rather dainty speedwell is found growing in small patches in drier areas on the meadow.

Tormentil

[rose family]

On first acquaintance this might be mistaken for a miniature buttercup, but its flowers have all the characteristics of a member of the rose family. It can be quite widespread in some of the drier areas which are also likely to be acidic.

Heath Bedstraw

[bedstraw family]

This is another plant associated with acidic soils, where it is fairly common, forming sprawling mats with its weak stems supported by the surrounding grasses. It is also another plant that is often considered rather 'ordinary', yet in an appropriate setting, such as this, has a charm all of its own. The 'frothy' clusters of flowers produce a rather sickly-sweet fragrance not dissimilar to that of meadow sweet.

Marsh Thistle

[daisy family]

A thistle found in places where the ground is damp or wet. Usually the stem lacks branches (as seen here) but has spiny winged outgrowths.

Spear Thistle

[daisy family]

A robust thistle that can grow to over a metre in height. Its name suits it well as the leaves possess long, piercingly sharp points. The flowers are commonly visited by butterflies.

Melancholy Thistle

[daisy family]

The plants of this unusual thistle spread by creeping runners and can cover large areas, often in damper ground.

The flowers usually occur singly at the end of tall, stout stems which may grow to over a metre. The plant is devoid of prickles and the leaves are quite distinctive, with the upper sides green and the undersides covered with short, white hairs giving them a downy appearance.

Flower head seen from above. Note that on this stem there is a second flower (bud).

Wild Thyme

[dead-nettle family]

An attractive plant with sprawling ground-hugging stems from which the short flowering shoots arise, bearing their pink flowers in clusters. These are a good source of nectar and are visited by a range of insects, especially bees. The whole plant produces essential oils which give rise to the characteristic aroma of thyme when the leaves are crushed.

Orchids

We have already encountered two members of the orchid family on the meadow and are now about to see the others. One feature of orchids is that flowering is unpredictable from year to year. All are perennials and store food materials in various underground devices, such as bulbs or swollen roots, that differ according to species. Some species, once mature, flower intermittently for a number of years. However many species flower only once and then die, depending solely on seed production for their continuance. A feature of the seed produced by all orchids is its diminutive size. When we sow familiar seeds in a garden or pot, given the right conditions, germination occurs quickly and the first green leaves soon appear; this is facilitated by seed food reserves. In the case of orchids, however, the very small seeds contain virtually no food store. In order to survive they need to be invaded by a parasitic fungus from the surrounding soil. This may seem a little curious; as gardeners know fungal parasites are not good news! In the case of orchids, however, this attack is resisted, the invading fungus is in part broken down to provide food material for the developing seedlings and the fungus confined to certain areas within a seed. In this battle the fortunes of the protagonists fluctuate during a year, with sometimes one and then the other dominating. A consequence of this is that orchid growth is extremely slow. Developing green leaves die down over winter and a number of years elapse before an orchid is sufficiently mature to produce flowers. This is one reason why orchid flowering is unpredictable.

Common Spotted-orchid

Contrary to the implication of the name of this orchid I have only ever come across limited numbers on the meadow. Plants are tall (up to 60 cm) in comparison to other species of orchids on the meadow, and they favour base-rich soils. This is a particularly fine spike of flowers.

125

Stretching the imagination somewhat it is perhaps possible to see the shape of a butterfly in each flower of the greater butterfly-orchid. These give off a sweet scent, and nectar is produced at the end of long spurs, which can only be reached by insects possessing long probosces. This is another plant associated with base-rich soils.

The small-white orchid, as its name suggests, has small white to creamy coloured flowers and these are arranged very close together on a spike often no more than 20 cm high. They produce a faint vanilla like scent. When growing amongst grasses this plant is easily overlooked. However, in this particular location, with low growing vegetation, it was quite conspicuous.

White flowers stand out particularly well at dusk and dawn. The greater butterfly-orchid is known to attract night-flying moths. Also the scent it produces is strongest at night.

126

Fragrant Orchid

The fragrant orchid is aptly named, for the attractive spikes of pale pink flowers are highly scented. When plants are found growing in compact groups, the scent can carry for some distance. This plant is found in grassland areas where the soil is base-rich.

Common Twayblade

Being all green, the common twayblade blends in with its surroundings and is one of those plants that can be easily missed.

Whilst seeds are produced, these orchids also produce buds on horizontal underground stems (rhizomes), thus providing an alternative means of dispersal.

The vernacular name relates to the pair of distinctive leaves that occur at the base of each plant.

128

Frog Orchid

The diminutive frog orchid is remarkably inconspicuous and difficult to spot. Even when one has been found, it is quite easy to lose it if one's attention is diverted to surrounding plants. There seem to be various suggestions regarding its common name; my own thought is that the lower lip of a flower looks like a frog's tongue when it is fully developed.

This is another orchid found in short grassland where the soil is probably base-rich.

Round-leaved Sundew

[sundew family]

Round-leaved sundew is the second of the two insectivorous plants found on the meadow. Typically it is found growing in association with the bog mosses, *Sphagnum* species, often on raised hummocks of the mosses.

The small white flowers of sundew are borne on spikes that frequently develop a curve at their ends; the flowers themselves seem quite reluctant to open to any extent. The rounded leaf blades occur at the end of long leaf stalks and are arranged in a basal rosette. The most obvious feature on the upper surface of the leaves is the presence of red hairs. These are glandular and each secretes a glistening, clear sticky droplet of fluid. These readily catch the light and, indeed, the name possibly derives from the fact that, unlike drops of dew, these do not dry up in sunlight. The hairs lying round the edge of a leaf are longer than those in the centre and are well placed to trap any insect that alights on them. What attracts insects to the leaves is not resolved with any degree of certainty – possibilities include simply their shiny nature or a possible resemblance to a source of nectar. However, once an insect (which can be as large as a damsel fly) is caught, and starts to struggle, the outer hairs bend inwards carrying the insect to the central part of the leaf where additional smaller, glandular hairs are located. These secrete a number of enzymes which break down the body of the prey and subsequently also absorb the released products of the digestion process, including nitrogenous compounds and mineral nutrients such as phosphate and potassium. These nutrients are important because in the acidic conditions associated with bog mosses, nitrogen in particular is in short supply because bacteria usually present in soil, which produce nitrogen in a form that can be absorbed by plant roots, are effectively inhibited by the prevailing acidity. Once the digestive process is complete the hairs bend outwards again and the chitin outer skeleton of the insect is eventually blown away.

Bog Mosses

[*Sphagnum* species]

Note the leaf of round-leaved sundew visible in the top right corner, showing the red hairs with glistening droplets.

Although there are no extensive areas of bog in the meadow, bog mosses are present in many of the wetter areas. Each bog moss plant bears groups of branches arising at the same level (node) on the stem. The nodes are closer together towards the apex of the stem and this creates a miniature 'mop head', a characteristic feature of bog mosses. The stems are usually vertical and closely packed together, creating moss mats. In some places the mosses grows above the (fluctuating) water level to form hummocks. The leaf of a bog moss is only one cell thick and can readily be examined under a microscope. As the photomicrograph shows, this reveals two types of cells. The larger are dead cells, held to their shape by bands of thickening. These are surrounded by smaller, thin living cells that contain chlorophyll and are usually green, although the green colour in some species is masked by the presence of a red pigment. Pores are present in the walls of the dead cell and water is absorbed through these, amounting in some cases to twenty to twenty-five times the dry weight of the plant. It is these cells that enable the moss to draw water upwards like a wick and thus continue to grow above the level of the water. Incidentally, bog mosses increase the acidity of their own environment by releasing hydrogen ions as a waste product in a cellular exchange process in which useful minerals are taken in. In common with other mosses, bog mosses disseminate spores as part of the reproductive cycle. The spores are produced within capsules, and the photograph shows such capsules early in their development; as they mature they are raised on short stalks above the level of the body off the moss. The spores are released when the top of a capsule blows of 'explosively'.

The photomicrograph of bog moss cells reveals an interesting pattern that I am sure a textile designer could utilize.

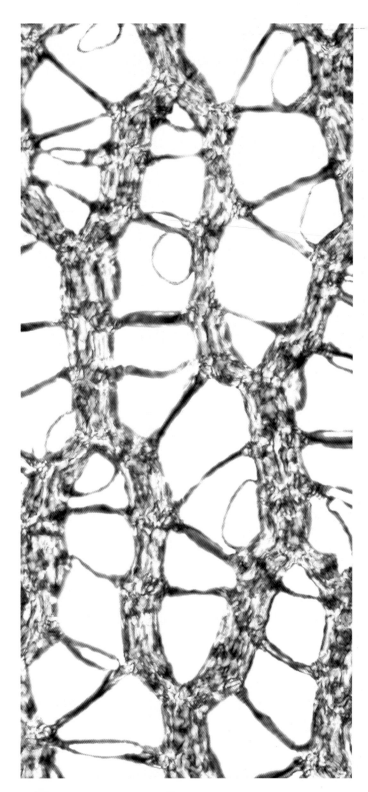

133

Common Frog

Frogs can be found in wetter grassland, usually not too far from water. Often their presence is given away when their movement disturbs the grass. In the open they move by jumping, using the power of their hind legs, but in very wet grass they use their legs to push through the stems. The latter mode is almost like swimming on land and frogs can move remarkably quickly in this way. More than once I have been surprised to find a frog rather than some other animal when I have detected movement.

Common Snipe

By the time July is reached, the calls of wading birds in particular have declined. One wader that is a consistent exception to this general rule is the common snipe. In the evening they can still be seen and heard drumming – a noise that sounds rather like a sheep bleating and is caused by air passing over two stiff tail feathers as a bird dives. On the ground common snipe make a repetitive, rather monotonous noise like an old fashioned sewing machine. Only rarely, however, do they make an appearance. They favour damp marshy ground and for the most part remain hidden (along with their nests) amongst the reed/sedge vegetation. I have never seen snipe chicks – perhaps one day?

135

Swallow

Swallows nest in nearby farm buildings and the adults patrol the grassland areas sweeping low as they trawl for insects. Their young can often be seen sitting around in trees, quite motionless, until suddenly perking up as an adult sweeps in to pass food whilst remaining on the wing.

Pheasant

Pheasants often put in an appearance. Whilst they are not wild birds as such, the cock birds make a splash of colour amongst the vegetation and strut about with an air of ownership of their domain, reinforced with an often repeated call.

Hen birds on the other hand blend in well with the surrounding vegetation, which can make them difficult to spot.

Meadow Pipit

Meadow pipits are generally quite numerous, both feeding and nesting in the shorter grassland. The male birds give notice of their territory by calling with a rather 'thin' song as they rise rapidly, and then this leads into a trill as they parachute down. In July the young birds in particular join up into groups of various sizes and seem to make a habit of perching on drystane dykes or the wire of a fence.

Song Thrush

Song thrushes nest in trees close to the grassland and quite openly go directly to and fro between the location of the nest and the feeding area.

As can be seen, they are capable of searching very successfully for worms.

Red Deer

In contrast to roe deer, red deer 'drop in' relatively rarely. In fact, I have only come across two stags during the many years of visiting the meadow.

This rather handsome stag looked as though he wanted to pose to be photographed, although the hind with him seemed very wary, as I have found with hinds elsewhere too.

Red Squirrel

Red squirrels frequent the adjacent Scots pine plantations but will venture across the fringes of the meadow to reach broad leaf trees that happen to be close by. If taken by surprise on such visits they may simply freeze but more often disappear down the 'blind' side of the tree trunk and beat a hasty retreat to the nearest conifers.

Roe Deer

By July the roe deer young (fawns), born in late May/early June, are well grown but still remain close to the doe. The doe is just out of the frame with the second young.

As can be seen the second fawn is still attempting to suckle.

Normally a doe will give birth to two fawns, as in this case, but mortality can be high.

[These shots were taken late in the evening. Just before the sun drops behind distant mountains the illumination has the intensity of a spot light. Then it fades rapidly as the sun disappears - just like stage lighting being extinguished.]

During July the roe buck are in peak condition as the time of the rut approaches. This particularly fine animal seemed oblivious to my presence; the fact that there was a doe nearby may have had something to do with this!

The mammals so far looked at have been herbivores. When it comes to carnivores, with a good supply of rabbits, hares and ground nesting birds available, one might anticipate foxes to be active. Over the years, however, I have only come across the droppings of a fox on one occasion and no kills that could be attributed to a fox. The most likely explanation is that foxes are well controlled locally.

Stoat and Weasel

Two small lithe hunters that do occur are the stoat and the weasel. In the summer they both have similarly coloured fur, a rather light brown on the upper part of the body and white/cream on the under surface. They operate in the same types of habitat, which usually overlap. This, together with the fact that they bound across ground with surprising speed and agility, can make them difficult to distinguish. The male stoat is larger than the female which is about the size of a male weasel. The female weasel is smaller than the male. As there is an overlap in size between the two species this cannot really be used to distinguish between them, and in any case gauging size is very difficult in the field situation. At reasonably close quarters a stoat can be positively identified by its tail, which has a black tip and is bushy, in contrast to that of the weasel which is quite short and smooth and lacks a black tip.

Both animals hunt over open ground, but seem to pay particular attention to drystane dykes where they will systematically enter crevices searching for prey. Stoats seem to prefer larger prey such as rabbits and have been recorded successfully tackling mountain hares. Weasels, certainly the females, can enter narrower crevices and tunnels than stoats and thus gain access to smaller rodents. However, there is considerable overlap in the prey species taken by both of these carnivores which, besides rodents, and given the opportunity, is likely to include eggs and young birds.

Both species have a natural curiosity which can be utilised to bring them close to an observer, a characteristic well used by gamekeepers! In my experience stoats never remain close for more than a short time. As these two photographs demonstrate, however, a weasel can apparently play hide and seek and stick its head out from time to time, in this case to be shot by a camera!

Common Lizard

On the drier grassland, when something scuttles at one's approach, disturbing the grass but remaining unseen, it is likely to be a lizard. They are remarkably quick and agile, but being cold blooded, they do bask in sunshine to bring their body temperature to a level at which their metabolic processes can function efficiently. Rocks and drystane dykes are commonly used as these reflect the absorbed warmth of incident radiation.

Where rocks are used with any degree of frequency, a giveaway is the droppings the lizards leave, like miniature bird droppings. One rock afforded me a good photo opportunity, although getting close enough was another matter. Along with good hearing and sense of smell, the sight of lizards is excellent and with anything but a painfully slow approach they vanish in an instant into a convenient crevice. When basking they simply cling to a suitable surface and remain absolutely motionless. The spreading five digits on their feet end in fine sharp claws, enabling them to climb walls as well as cling. When moving up or across steep surfaces they can also use their tails to provide additional stability.

Reptiles lay eggs, but the scientific name *Lacerta vivipara* suggests this lizard produces live young. It does in fact produce eggs, but these are retained within the body during development and maintained at the body temperature of the female. This may explain why this species can be found in more northern cooler regions than other egg laying lizards.

The colour of lizards is usually a mottling of browns although colouration can be variable. This one is darker than the norm.

[note there are two fresh droppings like those of birds.]

From time to time they shed their outer skin. Often this comes away in flakes, although in the photograph the impression is given that this particular lizard is shedding its skin from head to tail. The new skin is quite bright to start with, but dulls with age.

147

Flies

Various types of flies are present on the meadow. Collectively they make a significant contribution to the background 'buzz' of the grassland areas on warm days of high summer as well as attracting the attention with flight and colour.

Hover-flies visit various flowers in search of pollen and nectar. Their black and yellow banded bodies mimic well the body of a wasp, suggesting to likely predators that they can 'pack a punch' and should therefore be left alone.

Bumble-bee

Bumble-bees are present in noticeable numbers. They require a range of flowers in sufficient quantity to find nectar, for energy, and pollen, as a protein source, to maintain their numbers. For this reason they are regarded as good indicators of the health of an environment. The large hairy, dark-coloured, bodies of bumble-bees absorb and retain heat, allowing them to fly in dull conditions when other insects have ceased to be on the wing. This feature, plus the fact that pollen sticks to the hairs, makes them good pollinators.

White-tailed bumble-bee

Unlike honey bees, bumble-bee colonies are quite small and they produce insufficient honey for a colony to survive overwinter. In the autumn, however, newly mated queen bees do possess sufficient food reserves to hibernate. On emerging in the spring a queen lays eggs in a nest to start a new colony. The nests of some species are underground in, for example, old mouse tunnels. The white-tailed bumble-bee uses an underground nest. Others, including the common carder bee, create nests above ground at the base of grasses. When foraging a bumble-bee sucks up nectar, with mouth parts that may be likened to a straw, and this is stored in a 'bag' in the abdomen, know as a 'honey stomach'. When full it can account for at least 50% of the body weight of the bee. Periodically a bee will comb pollen off its body and store it in pollen baskets on its hind legs.

Common carder bee

The name for this small bumblebee relates to the way it builds a nest by 'knitting' together vegetation close to the ground. Note the well filled pollen basket on its hind leg.

149

Common Blue Damselfly

Sawfly

At certain times areas of long grass seem to attract the common blue damsel fly. Whilst these are quite small, with thin bodies, the black and blue colours of the male make them easily spotted in flight. (The females have grey-green and black bodies.) The wings move independently of each other. At first sight this can give the impression of a weak, dithering flight. However, this feature actually provides them with the manoeuvrability of a helicopter when chasing prey. They can move slowly forward or dart at speed as well as hover. Having caught a small insect they then settle on a piece of vegetation. It is interesting to watch the meticulous way they first strip off the wings and then the legs before consuming the body of the prey.

Whilst photographing the common blue damselfly I was aware of something entering my peripheral vision. It was this sawfly. I managed to refocus and take one shot before it disappeared as quickly as it had come. Sawflies have a wasp-like head but, unlike wasps, their bodies are not waisted. Most sawflies feed on pollen, though this particular member of the sawfly group hunts mostly for small flies and has been recorded as taking prey as large as a damsel fly. The name sawfly relates to the female ovipositor. This is used to cut into vegetation before laying eggs.

Golden Ringed Dragonfly

Blue damselflies are likely to be overlooked, but it is impossible to miss the rapid and erratic movements of the golden-ringed dragonfly. Whilst the movements may at first seem erratic and random, if a watch is kept from one particular position it will soon become apparent that they have a definite 'beat' which they patrol repeatedly. They have very well developed compound eyes and are adept at catching insects as they 'hawk' over their patch of ground. When they do settle, they hang down from some chosen piece of vegetation with their wings outstretched. For an insect that is so prominently marked, it is remarkable how they can 'vanish' when they settle, even if watched with great care. Frequently, when trying carefully to approach the place where I knew one had settled I have only succeeded in putting it up before spotting where it was. However, when successfully approached, they often remain on their chosen vegetation for quite a while, giving ample opportunity to take a photograph.

[In contrast to the damselflies in which, when at rest, the wings lie parallel to the body and fold over the top of the abdomen, the wings of dragonflies remain outstretched at right angles to their bodies.]

Grasshoppers

The chirping stridulation of grasshoppers is a sound that, perhaps more than any other in the insect world, evokes the feeling of high summer in grassland (although not all grasshoppers can produce this sound).

Grasshopper species show variation in colour. The colours of the common green grasshopper range from a bright green to olive-brown. Usually there is some green on the body but males may be all brown, as exemplified by this specimen.

Common Green Grasshopper

Meadow Grasshopper

The fore-wings of meadow grasshoppers are reduced and their hind wings vestigial and cannot support them in sustained gliding, as is the case for other grasshopper species. This one is voiding small pellets, the remains of the grasses on which it has been feeding.

No summer period would be complete without the presence of butterflies adding their particular style of movement, and often the bonus of bright colours, to the meadow. July and August are the best months to see them.

Quite a few species frequent the area over these two months; most are fairly common, but one or two have a more limited distribution. Apart from the many types of flowers providing nectar, crucially, the range of plants available can provide food for the larvae of a number of species.

July butterflies

Meadow Brown

The meadow brown is very approachable and does not readily take to flight. It may be found feeding on a variety of flowers, but in common with a number of species seems to favour thistles and knapweeds. The larvae feed on a variety of grasses. The under sides of the wings of both sexes show large false eyes as seen in the above pair.

The colour of a male is dark brown. This specimen is rather faded, suggesting it is an ageing individual.

Common Blue

This species is widespread throughout Britain.

The upper wings of the male are a brilliant blue, edged with a white border. The blue coloration is caused by the fact that the scales absorb all the spectrum colours of light except blue, which they reflect.

In this region the females have a line of orange coloured chevrons bordering the outer wing edges, while the rest of the wings are blue rendering the female a showier butterfly than the male. This colour form is particularly prevalent in Scotland. (In more southern regions of the UK a darkish brown predominates, with some infusion of blue.)

In the early morning these butterflies may often be found on bare ground, taking in mineral salts dissolved in water provided by overnight dew.

Many butterflies simply seem to disappear as evening approaches. However, blues can commonly be found on grass stems with their wings closed and heads pointing downwards, a situation that provides an opportunity to examine the attractive markings on the under wings.

The larvae of the common blue feed on a variety of plants from the pea family – a good range of these is available in the meadow, bird's-foot-trefoil being the commonest.

Northern Brown Argus

The northern brown argus is classed as a member of the family of blue butterflies, but in this instance both males and females have brown coloured wings. Orange chevrons, as seen in the female common blue, are present on the outer wing margins of both sexes. If it were not for the fact that in this area the female common blues have blue wings it would be quite possible at a distance to mistake this butterfly for a brown female common blue. However, closer to, the distinctive white spot on the forewing of the argus confirms the identification. In contrast to the common blue, this butterfly has a fairly restricted range. being found mainly in hilly northern areas on base-rich soils where the larval food plant, the common rock rose, is available.

Ringlet

The ringlet is dark brown in colour. When it settles to feed it typically closes its wings revealing the feature from which its name derives: clearly visible eye-spots (usually) on the undersurface of its wings. Each eye-spot has a white middle surrounded by a black ring which in turn is surrounded by a yellow one. Whilst the upper wing surfaces are described as looking like velvet the under surfaces, to my mind, have the appearance of a brushed fabric. On the meadow they fly over the open meadow, though in more southerly areas of the UK they tend to be associated with damp areas and the shade of woodland.

The eye-spots can vary in shape from circular to elongated. In this unusual (aberrant) specimen they are reduced to barely visible small white dots.

A time of transition
(August)

As July gives way to August we find that many of the plants flowering in the previous month continue to do so well into this month. Also, there are some plants which seem to come to the fore at this time, or which we see flowering for the first time. However, we can find an increasing number of plants that are past their best. Many are in the process of setting seed, or have already done so, and this gives an end of season atmosphere to the meadow.

Curlew

Flowers and seeding.

By the time August is reached the calls of wading birds, in particular, have declined. A fact that is suddenly brought to our attention as the silence of a peaceful evening is interrupted by the call of a lone curlew flying over.

Lady's Bedstraw

[bedstraw family]

Lady's bedstraw has a long flowering period which starts in June and may extend well into September. When other plants are no longer vying for attention, the small, bright, clear yellow flowers, born in clusters up the stem, are distinctly eye-catching. The stems are quite spindly and to attain any height they have to rely on nearby grasses for support, otherwise they sprawl and flower more or less at ground level. Plants spread by means of underground stems and as a result recover readily from grazing. Another attraction of this plant is that the flowers produce a heady, honey-sweet scent.

Yarrow

[daisy family]

At first sight the large rather flat flower heads of yarrow do not immediately suggest 'daisy', but close examination of the numerous small flowers comprising each head reveals a typical daisy family structure with both disc and ray florets. The colour of the flowers can vary from white to pink (this specimen is the pinkest I have ever come across) and the heads are borne on thick stems. In contrast, the leaves are finely divided, a feature that is reflected in the specific name *'millifolium'* (a thousand leaf).

Harebell, (Scottish Bluebell)

[bellflower family]

The harebell, commonly known as bluebell in Scotland, is another plant with creeping underground stems from which vertical stems arise and bear attractive lantern-like flowers varying in colour from a very light to deep blue. They are usually found in drier parts of grassy areas, but do not seem to be fussy regarding the type of soil.

Eyebright

[figwort family]

At this time of year eyebright can be the dominant plant is some places. In this photograph it is growing on a covered old tree stump (left hand half of the picture.)

Eyebright is found mainly in drier areas of the grassland and is another plant that is a hemiparasite. Its maximum height is 150 cm and the small flowers vary from white to purple.

There is a large number of very similar species of eyebright and it requires an expert botanist to identify what species a particular plant is. This task is not helped by the fact that they freely hybridise!

Slender St John's-wort

[St John's wort family]

The slender St John's-wort seems to prefer drier ground. It is a graceful plant with rich yellow flowers and tinges of red. Whilst it starts flowering in the early summer, its continuing presence in August makes a welcome addition to the flora at this time.

Common Knapweed

[daisy family]

The round developing flower heads of the common knapweed are extremely hard, giving rise to the apt and popular alternative name of 'hardhead'.

The reddish thistle-like flowers seem to provide a good food source for insects at this time or year, judging by the number commonly found on them.

Goldenrod

[daisy family]

Goldenrod is a plant that often seems not to put in an appearance until August, with the flowers not being at their best until late in the month, if they have not been eaten in the meantime. There have been several occasions when I had noted the position of promising plants only to find the flower heads taken by some herbivore whilst still in bud!

Bush Vetch

[pea family]

The bush vetch is in many ways rather inconspicuous as it scrambles through grasses, hanging on with its tendrils. It seems to have a long flowering season, but is perhaps most readily noticed in August when there are not so many other plants competing for attention. When examined close to, the purplish-blue flowers are most attractive.

Heather

[heather family]

The plant most commonly associated with the 'glorious twelfth' is, of course, the heather since it produces its annual carpet of purple at this time. There are patches of ground on the meadow that suit heather well, though it is never so dense that other plants are excluded.

Another example of a single species growing on an old tree stump; in this instance a visible one.

Flowers in close up.

168

Along with heather there are two other members of the heather family present on the meadow. Though they can be found growing close together they occupy quite different soil conditions.

Bell Heather

This was found on a dryish, raised area surrounded by much damper soil, which was distinctly boggy in places. Other sites for this heather are also on drier, well drained soils. Whilst this was photographed in August, bell heather starts flowering during July and has an extended flowering period.

Cross-leaved Heath

As can be seen from the photograph, this was growing on the edge of shallow standing water; a typical location.

169

Yellow Saxifrage

[saxifrage family]

During this month some of the wetter base-rich areas are host to the delightful yellow saxifrage.

Flowers in close up.

The clear yellow flowers of the saxifrage plants can spread out over expansive wet areas (above) and also highlight concealed channels, as illustrated in the photograph to the right.

171

Devil's-bit Scabious

[teasel family]

[seen here with yellow saxifrage.]

The devil's-bit scabious starts to flower in August and is in full flower from the middle of the month onwards, continuing well into September. The bluish-purple flower heads, each packed with numerous small individual flowers, are borne on long stems. So what looks like a single flower head is in fact a compound flower which might at first sight be taken for a member of the daisy family, but on close examination the flowers are seen to have a very different structure.

The common name for this plant is a little unusual. Apparently the Devil was so infuriated by the range of ills that this plant was reputed to cure that he bit off part of the root stock. The roots do give the appearance of having been bitten off, but the reason for this is obscure and is more likely to be an evolutionary trait than the work of the Devil!

172

Quaking-grass

[grass family]

Quaking-grass, which flowers from early summer to the end of August, is aptly named: its attractive flower heads are attached to thin wire-like stalks that cause them to 'dance' in even the slightest suggestion of a breeze. It is most often found associated with other plants that seem to prefer a base-rich soil.

Viviparous Sheep's-fescue

[grass family]

This grass is very similar to sheep's-fescue, However, instead of producing flowers followed by seeds, it forms minute plantlets in the flower head. These, with miniature blades of grass, become detached and grow into new plants.

173

Field Gentian

[gentian family]

Whilst the flowering times of most plants on the meadow are fairly predictable, that of the field gentian can vary from year to year. My records show that sometimes it appears in July and is almost over by the beginning of August, although in most years it is a very welcome addition to the August flora.

Occasionally a 'white' form may be found, although careful examination reveals the white to be suffused with a pink/blue hue.

174

Grass-of-Parnassus

[saxifrage family]

Undoubtedly the 'flower of the month' has to be the graceful grass-of-Parnassus, found only in a few isolated, rather boggy locations.

Close examination of an individual flower shows that there are five stamens that are fertile and five that are sterile. The latter each split into five fine fingers, ending in shiny yellow globules. It is surmised that these attract insects, but in fact offer no reward.

175

Stag's-horn Clubmoss

Previously we have seen the ground-hugging stem of a stag's-horn club moss. This photograph (taken in very dull and damp conditions) shows a fertile vertical stem bearing the typical twin 'cones' in which spores develop.

Lesser Clubmoss

The very small lesser clubmoss also produces vertical fertile stems from others that creep over the ground. The spore-containing structures (sporangia) can be seen at the bases of upper leaves.

Hard-fern

This fern, which is found where the soil tends to be acidic, differs in one or two respects from other ferns that we have seen. For example, the basal rosette of leaves (fronds) is quite robust and does not die back at the end of a season but persists from year to year. These are non-fertile (do not produce spores).

Also, each year new, fertile, vertical leaves are produced with much narrower leaflets (pinnules) than those on the basal leaves. Their arrangement looks rather ladder like. The spore bearing structures are on the under-surfaces of these leaflets and once the spores have been shed, the fertile fronds die back.

August butterflies

During this month butterflies seem in particular to favour creeping thistles and the devil's-bit scabious.

Tortoiseshell

This tortoiseshell is feeding on creeping thistle. Indeed, tortoiseshells seem generally to prefer thistles to the exclusion of almost all other flowers and it is not unusual to find several near to each other on a patch of this plant. The larvae feed on nettles, then hibernate over winter as adults, commonly hiding away in farm buildings.

Red Admiral

The red admiral, when not feeding, seems to 'enjoy' finding somewhere, such as bare ground or a fence post, to settle and spread out its wings when the sun is shining.

The UK population of this butterfly is swollen considerably during spring by immigrants from continental Europe. Later many of the summer hatch of butterflies migrate south in the autumn. The larvae feed on nettles.

Peacock

The peacock butterfly is well named as it is very colourful and has large 'false eyes' that resemble the patterns in the tail feathers of the peacock bird. It has the habit of opening and closing its wings quite quickly when approached. Presumably this is a defence mechanism to try to ward off a predator, but can be frustrating for the photographer! The undersides of the wings are very dark and when closed can make it difficult to see this butterfly in many situations. Like the tortoiseshell, larvae of the peacock feed on nettles, while the adults hibernate over winter in farm buildings or even in crevices or the hollow parts of trees.

Green-veined White

The green-veined white is by far the commonest white butterfly in this area. The name derives from the fact that the veins, when seen from the underside of a wing, are highlighted by a particular concentration of both black and yellow scales, the combination giving a greenish appearance. This seems to show up most clearly when the wings are at least partly backlit.

Green-veined whites are commonly found in damper areas and can frequently be seen feeding on the flowers of ragged robin. (In the intense direct sunlight of this photograph, the greenish appearance of the veins has not recorded.)

The larvae feed on lady's smock, another plant of boggy ground.

Painted Lady

As the name painted lady suggests, this butterfly is indeed attractive and colourful. They are long distance travellers, migrating to Scotland from as far away as continental Europe and North Africa. The eggs and larvae, the latter feeding on nettles and thistles, produce a second generation of adults.

Many migrate south in the autumn; any that fail to do so are unlikely to survive the winter in this area, although in southern parts of the UK some may find a suitable place to hibernate.

Dark Green Fritillary

The dark green fritillary is another butterfly that seems to prefer thistles, commonly tall ones. This can make it very visible although, even when feeding, it is not the easiest of butterflies to approach. More often than not it will take off just out of photographic range, disappearing into the far distance with a rapid and powerful flight.

The photograph shown below was taken towards the end of August when this particular individual seemed quite lethargic, probably being slightly intoxicated, for at this time of year the nectar can start to ferment in the flowers!

The larvae feed on violet leaves.

Scotch Argus

The Scotch argus is another butterfly that it is closely associated with hill and mountain areas. Its preferred habitat is damp long grass and eggs are commonly laid on purple moor grass. Whilst its flight looks quite lazy, it is easily disturbed and will take off well ahead of anyone walking through its grassy domain, even when the sun is not shining or in the cool of the evening.

Moths

The great majority of moths are nocturnal. Since my work on the meadow was always carried out during daylight hours, I am unaware of the range of species of moth that may be present. However the two species shown here are ones that I came across on a regular basis during daylight hours. Depending on their size, moths are grouped rather arbitrarily into micro-moths and macro-moths.

Plume moth

This is a micro-moth, whose name relates to its rather feathery wings. This individual was tricky to photograph as it was vibrating its body with only very short pauses. Moths can do this to 'warm up' before flight or, in the case of females, to waft a pheromone to attract a mate.

Antler moth

This is a macro-moth. The cream coloured, horizontal strip in the middle of the wing forks to the rear. This is fancifully likened to an antler, although it is not particularly obvious in this specimen. They are very active during the day and in some years occur in large numbers.

Birds

With the departure of the summer visitors and their young there are fewer species of birds to be seen in August. Those that remain are perhaps more readily noticed at this time. Crows remain very much in evidence, various tits can be seen exploring cones on the conifers, and mistle thrushes continue to feed in the grassland.

Greylag geese regularly fly over the meadow to and from the nearby loch.

Treecreeper

During August, when there are fewer plants to photograph, there is more time in a day to simply observe. On one such occasion I spotted this treecreeper working its way up the trunk of a tree, prising out insects with it finely curved 'tooth pick' of a bill. Having reached the upper part of the tree it then flew to the base of another to start the process again. This is characteristic behaviour of a treecreeper.

Kestrel

Kestrels may often be seen hovering at a distance, but eventually I came across one observing from a perch. This is either an adult female or a juvenile.

186

Buzzard

Buzzards can still be seen effortlessly circling as they survey the ground for likely prey. When not doing so they seem to disappear for long periods, although I suspect that often I am unaware of being observed from some vantage point in a tree. This time luck was on my side and I managed to locate one.

Tawny Owl

Tawny owls roost during the day, usually perching close to the trunk on a branch of a tree. I had been watching this one for some twenty minutes before trying to take a photograph; it seemed to be enjoying the sunshine and was frequently moving its head to look around, including checking me out!

187

Roe Deer Rut

One August I was scanning part of the meadow with a pair of binoculars late in the evening when I spotted a roe deer doe, and then realised that a buck was in attendance. The doe was grazing, seemingly taking no particular notice of the buck. When she had moved a short distance, the buck would move up and then lay down again. This behaviour was repeated over and over again, the buck looking for all the world like a working sheep dog!

After quite some time it became apparent that the doe was moving in the direction of the crest of a slope, with the buck still in attendance and still keeping his distance, moving and then lying down for a while as he had been doing since I first observed them. I swapped the binoculars for my camera and telephoto lens and headed for a wall running close to the crest, crouching down to keep my profile below the wall. For once my luck was in, there being little wind to carry my scent. Roe deer have an acute sense of both smell and hearing. I was concerned about the noise of the camera shutter, but there was some activity in the distance, caused by people returning to their car, and this drew the deers' attention. First the doe came by and disappeared and then the buck; a few moments to savour.

I have seen, on a number of occasions, the well recorded behaviour of a buck chasing a doe round in a circle, but not on this meadow. However, this was the first and so far only time I have witnessed a buck tracking a doe in this unusual manner.

189

Autumn: bright colours and fruitfulness
(September and October)

As August gives way to September and then October, the flowering season is virtually at an end. The 'spent' grasses in particular begin to give the area something of an untidy appearance as they lose much of their colour and flop about. However, as can be seen from the photograph, the devil's-bit scabious continues flowering for a good part of September and is thus the plant that draws the flowering season to a conclusion

Although the main 'season' for fungi starts in August, the familiar forms of mushrooms and toadstools are most in evidence during September and October. One of the many fascinating things about fungi is the highly variable range of structures and colours their 'fruiting bodies' present.

Although visible throughout the year, lichens also have a fungal component. So now is perhaps an opportune time to take a closer look at these as well, while there is less to divert our attention but before it gets too cold!

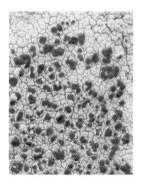

During September and into October, as plants begin to shut down in preparation for the now imminent winter season, not only are means of propagation as seeds and fruits completed, but we are provided with a spectacular blaze of colour as greens give way to a variety of yellow, brown and red hues.

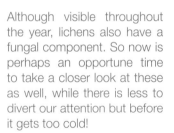

Fungi

The familiar mushrooms and toadstools are the fruiting bodies, or reproductive structures, of fungi and produce vast numbers of spores that disseminate these organisms. When they germinate, the spores produce very fine clear threads (hyphae) that grow through whatever proves to be a suitable food source. Collectively, these threads form an interweaving network (mycelium) that can be thought of as the 'body' of the fungus.

At certain times in a year, usually autumn, an area of mycelium will coalesce to form a dense mass, which then develops into a highly visible fruiting body, as seen here.

Scarlet Wax Cap

The newly emerging fruiting body of the scarlet wax cap is indeed a bright scarlet. However, as it matures and increases in size, the colour changes to a yellow hue.

Downward projecting 'gills' occur under the top surfaces (caps) of many mushrooms and toadstools. These can be clearly seen on the mature scarlet wax cap. Spores are formed on the sides of gills.

Many fungi form relationships with the roots of a diversity of plants. For example, it has been estimated that more than eighty percent of 'higher' (vascular) plants form such mycorrhizal associations. In mycorrhizas the mycelium of the fungus involved forms a dense mesh that encompasses the plant roots. Individual hyphal threads of the mycelium then grow some distance into the surrounding soil and in doing so sweep a much greater volume of soil for nutrients than the roots of the plant can.

Boletus species

The feature that characterises the bolete group of fungi is that spores are not produced in gills but rather in small vertical tubes packed very closely together on the underside of a cap. This gives the underside surface a rather sponge like appearance. Apart from this distinction, they have many similar characteristics to gill bearing fungi.

The growing tips of the hyphae of mycorrhizal fungi secrete digestive enzymes into their immediate environment and these break down surrounding materials to their simple component elements that are then absorbed and either used by the fungus or passed on to the plant partner. This is natural recycling and fungi, together with bacteria, play a key role in this essential process. Without it, all the spent grasses and other plant material, as well as animal waste and dead bodies, would remain intact and the elements utilised in their formation be 'locked up' as a result. Effectively they would be taken out of circulation. The activities of fungi and bacteria liberate these component elements for reuse. The mineral nutrients, such as phosphorus, and water, absorbed by the fungal hyphae and passed to the plant partner are thus directly recycled. Indeed, some trees and orchids are unable to grow without a mychorrizal partner. These associations are not all one way, however: fungi lack chlorophyll, but instead are able to 'tap' the energy rich photosynthetic products of their partner plants. Such mutually beneficial relationships are referred to as symbiotic.

Fly Agaric

This fungus, familiar from illustrations in many story books for children, was found close to a birch, a tree with which this species of fungus commonly forms a mychorrizal association.

The fungi we have seen so far have had fruiting bodies of the toadstool pattern - a cap borne on a stem (stipe). However, fungi are not limited to this pattern, as examples from the meadow on this page and the next illustrate. Where they are club-shaped or spindle-shaped spores are produced on the outside of the upper surfaces.

Earth Tongue

Smoky Spindles

195

Yellow Fan

Common Puffball

Spores are produced in puffballs on the inner surface of the 'ball'. A pore develops on the top of the fruiting body and pressure on the surface of the 'ball' causes spores to puff out in clouds. Animal contact, raindrops or gusts of wind can all cause a discharge of spores.

196

Some fungi invade trees and cause disease, and these commonly produce fruiting bodies that project like brackets from the trunk, hence the name bracket fungi. Their presence is not good news as it indicates that the interior of a tree is being attacked and will soon rot.

Razor Strop Fungus*
[The photograph was taken in July]

This is a cause of disease on birch trees and is only found on this host. The young fruiting body is creamy white with a smooth surface, but with age it will develop a much rougher texture.

Porcelain Fungus

This is restricted to beech trees. It is a glistening white due to the presence of a sticky mucilage on its surface

Certain fungi specialise in growing on dung, which on the meadow is either from cattle (mainly) or sheep. Such fungi are said to be 'coprophilic' and are involved in recycling. They assist, along with other organisms, in the breakdown of the dung and the release of nutrients back into the soil. Other organisms involved include bacteria and the larvae of various flies, such as the dung-fly.

Snowy Inkcap

Mottle Gill

198

Brownie species

Lichens

Lichens have appeared in many of the previous photographs. They can be almost like wallpaper; simply there in the background. However, a closer look reveals an absorbing range of patterns and colours. Unlike many plants, they are present all the year round and for the most part look more or less the same whatever the time of year. They are of interest, too, in that they survive extremes of temperature and varying conditions of water availability.

There are no formally agreed vernacular names for lichens. Difficulties arise when a species has more than one common name or a single name is used for more than one species. For this reason scientific names should alway be used..

Lichens are categorised into three basic growth forms. In crustose lichens, as the name implies, the thallus is crust-like; in fruticose lichens, the thallus is shrubby/club-like or hanging; and in foliose lichens the thallus is leaf or scale-like.

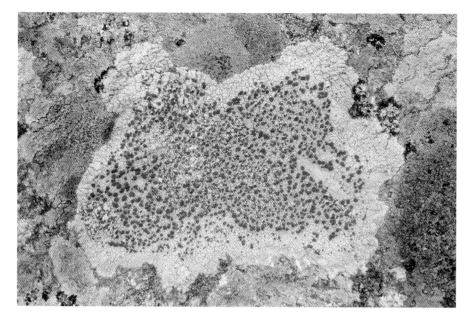

Ophioparma ventosa
[crustose]

Cladonia diversa
[fructicose]

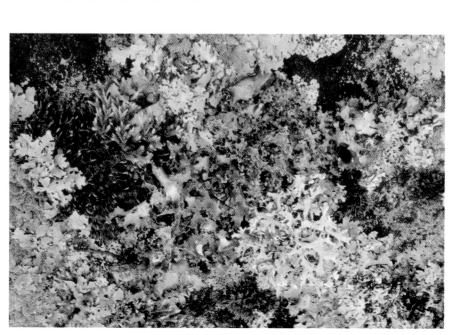

Platismatia glauca (main subject)
[foliose]

A lichen consists of a combination of two types of organism, an alga and a fungus. Both seem to benefit from the arrangement (another example of a symbiotic relationship), although it may not be a truly equal partnership. The algal partner is either a green alga (green algae have a photosynthetic pigments similar to those found in plants), or a member of the blue-green algae (these are bacteria which possess photosynthetic pigments which differ from those of the green algae).

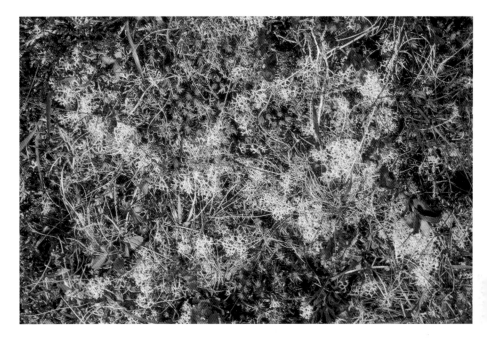

Cladonia portentosa
[fructicose]

A name commonly used for this lichen is 'reindeer moss'. This illustrates the problem of using vernacular names, because firstly it is not a moss, and secondly there is another *Cladonia* species also referred to as reindeer moss.

It seems that the fungal partner determines the characteristic appearance of the lichen and gains energy-rich carbon compounds produced by the photosynthetic activity of the algal partner. It is probable that the alga gains some protection from environmental extremes of heat and cold by being embedded under a dense upper layer of fungal hyphae. This may also give some protection from excessive radiation, in particular UV light. Also, the algal partner gains mineral nutrients from the associated fungus, which in turn gains some of these from its immediate environment, but mainly from the surrounding air and rainfall. It is this, incidentally, that renders lichens so sensitive to atmospheric pollution.

Cladonia polydactyla
[fructicose]

201

One characteristic of lichens is that they can both dry out and rehydrate extremely rapidly. When desiccated, the algal component goes into 'suspended animation' and the photosynthetic system effectively switches off. The process readily reverses when moisture becomes available. It is this ability that allows them to grow, albeit slowly, in such difficult environments.

The fungi associated with lichens produce what are referred to as 'lichen acids' and some of these are pigmented. It is these pigments that provide the varied colours associated with lichens and which are sometimes utilised as a source of natural dyes.

Lecanora gangaleoides
[crustose]

Caloplaca flavovirescens
[crustose]

This photograph shows part of a drystane dyke on which a number of crustose lichens are growing, including:

Lecidea lithophila: this is the partially rusty coloured one on the central stone.

Rhizocarpon geographicum: this is the bright green one on the surrounding stones. It does have the widely used common name of map lichen, due to its appearance which can be likened to that of old maps.

Autumn Colours

We can now take the opportunity to look at a selection of plants and see how they add another visual dimension to the meadow at this time of year.

Birch

A stand of mainly birch.

Even an old veteran birch can add to the aesthetic appeal.

Bilberry

The various hues of autumnal colours are due to a range of pigments. Carotinoids (as found in carrots) are present all the time but the colours are masked by the presence of the green pigment chlorophyll. They are revealed, however, when the chlorophyll starts to break down in autumn. The breakdown products are moved to other parts of a plant, such as the roots, where they are stored over winter to be utilised again in new leaves the following spring. Another group of pigments, the anthocyanins, are produced at this time and these lead to additional colours.

Bog Asphodel

The seed heads of bog asphodel positively glow in autumn sunshine.

Deergrass

[sedge family]

This grass seems to set the meadow on fire with the brilliance of its colours.

Dog-rose

The brilliant red of the dog-rose hips, which are bursting with seeds, attract a variety of seed eating birds. The seeds themselves are eventually disseminated over a large area in bird droppings.

Wild Cherry

The colourful wild cherries soon go when they are ripe, but the leaves remain eventually to add yet more colour to the meadow.

Rowan

[rose family]

The young rowan is providing a splash of colour in a bed of mosses, as it attempts to establish itself.

208

As a young buzzard keeps a look out from a vantage point in an old downy birch, surrounded by the splendour of autumn colours, it will soon learn that the season can change almost overnight.

The winter months
(November to March)

An approaching snowstorm

By the beginning of November the deciduous trees have shed their leaves and the meadow is facing the onset of winter. However, the winter months are far from being devoid of interest.

An audible indicator that winter has truly arrived is the trumpeting call of the whooper swans, as they arrive from their breeding grounds in Iceland. The birds are visible from the meadow as mere white dots on the nearby loch but their ornithological 'yodelling' calls echo between the hills and across the meadow.

The winter months can be a time of contrasts.

Black Grouse

These black grouse dropped in when I was out walking one day in the December sunshine.

On other occasions the grip of the winter months can be both bleak and awe inspiring.

Sparrow
Hawk

Whilst motoring along the meadow road one day in January, I witnessed this bird of prey fell a partridge and then carry it some distance before settling to eat its carcass, fortunately still close to the road. The road was down hill and I managed to coast slowly along and pull off onto the verge, with the bird in range of a telephoto lens. It took twenty minutes to dismember the partridge and I was able to take a series of photographs. Whilst this event does not fit my usual genre of photography, it was nevertheless interesting from a behaviour point of view; in particular the meticulous way it plucked the breast feathers from its kill.

Hooper Swan

As we have seen during the winter months this nearby loch is frequented by hoopers. If the loch becomes largely frozen over many of them disperse. The relatively small area of water immediately adjacent to the meadow may remain unfrozen, possibly due to a through flow of water. Some swans may be found here and can be easily viewed from an edge of the meadow.

In this situation it can be seen that they move about as family groups.

The narrow meadow road runs close to the edge of this water (between the swans and my vantage point) and is frequented by hill walkers. Normally, both the parents and the cygnets would move around quite freely whilst feeding on submerged vegetation. However, as soon as walkers come along they bunch into a tight knit group, adopting a defensive posture.

215

Mountain (Blue) Hare

In the spring we saw a mountain hare shedding its winter coat and then, later, the brown summer coat. Incidentally, besides the spring moult to brown fur there is a second moult which starts around mid-summer and can continue into September. As this coat is also brown, it in effect means that this moult is inconspicuous, in contrast to the third moult to the winter coat. The appearance of the winter coat starts in October and can continue until December/January. Whilst a mountain hare usually appears white at a distance, the extent to which it is pure white can be very variable. Closer to it is quite common to find browns and/or grey colours present. The fully formed winter coat does not seem to last very long as the process soon goes into reverse, with the head starting to turn brown again first.

When running the mountain hare has a more bouncing gait than a brown hare, which serves it well over the type of terrain it commonly traverses. Also, it has longer hind legs in proportion to its body size than the brown and the feet are broader, again a useful feature for movement over soft ground or snow.

This animal losing its winter coat was spotted in March, some distance away on a hill side and I wondered if I could work my way towards it to get within a reasonable shooting distance. Luck was on my side as a herd of cows started to pass between myself and the hare. In good 'army fashion' I decided to use them like tanks to act as shields, whilst gradually moving forwards complete with long lens on a tripod. It worked, I got within shooting distance and managed to take a number of photographs. However, the hare kept moving about as it continued to feed rather casually, which made things a little tricky. It did take a good look at me but did not seem concerned.

Then flashing information in the viewfinder told me I had finished the film, at which point I realised that my spare film was in the camera bag some distance behind me! I left the lens plus tripod and tried to crawl backwards, watching the hare all the time, but unfortunately failed to navigate safely past all the fresh cowpats! However, I did manage to crawl back again with more film and by this time the hare was dozing in the late afternoon sun and seemed oblivious to my presence. It was still there when I got back to my camera bag and walked away.

Epilogue

We are now approaching full circle in our year on the meadow. The appearance of brown on the face of the mountain hare is a hint that the winter season is well past its mid-way point, though it may not feel like that! By March, however, other subtle changes start to appear as, for example, the flush of colour in the branches of the larch and birch trees as the sap starts to rise.

At various points during this journey through the seasons, reference has been made to the presence of farm animals. These are some of the cattle which have over wintered on the meadow and soon they will be moved to the foot hills of the mountains for the summer season.

The floristic richness of the meadow owes a great deal to the presence of the farm animals. They graze on the vegetation, mainly during the late autumn, winter and early spring, This prevents grasses from becoming rank and competing with other plants for light. With only occasional light grazing during the rest of the year, the flowering plants are able to grow, store food reserves and set seed before significant grazing recommences. Also the animals play an additional important role in that, through their dung, plant nutrients are both recycled and redistributed.

Purple
Saxifrage

[saxifrage family]

A worthwhile detour in April is to follow the cattle onto the foothills in order to see this early flowering gem. It is found associated with a small area of limestone.

Back on the meadow, coltsfoot, creeping willow, wood anemones, primroses and dog violets will be heralding the start of a new season and somewhere out there will be a brown hare (possibly our original one). So the circle is complete and after twelve months, whilst we have returned to the starting point of our excursion, it is not an end but simply another beginning.

As I now reflect on the years and time spent on this meadow, as well as the privilege of access afforded to both Joy and myself, I still find it difficult to realise that this is farmland, not a nature reserve: a fact, I feel, that is worth taking time to ponder upon.

Appendices

A) **Scientific names for the illustrated flowering plants**

Anemone, Wood	*Anemone nemorosa*	Goldenrod	*Solidago virgaurea*
Asphodel, Bog	*Narthecium ossifragum*	Grass-of-Parnassus	*Parnassia palustris*
Asphodel, Scottish	*Tofieldia pusilla*	Harebell (Scottish bluebell)	*Campanula rotundifolia*
Avens, Water	*Geum rivale*	Heath, Cross-leaved	*Erica tetralix*
Bartsia, Red	*Odontites vernus*	Heather	*Calluna vulgaris*
Bedstraw, Heath	*Galium saxatile*	Heather, Bell	*Erica cinerea*
Bedstraw, Lady's	*Galium verum*	Knapweed, Common	*Centaurea nigra*
Beech	*Fagus sylvatica*	Lady's-mantle	*Alchemilla sp.*
Bilberry	*Vaccinium myrtillus*	Lousewort	*Pedicularis sylvatica*
Birch, Downy	*Betula pubescens*	Lousewort, Marsh	*Pedicularis palustris*
Bird's-foot-trefoil, Common	*Lotus corniculatus*	Marsh-marigold	*Caltha palustris*
Bistort, Alpine	*Persicaria vivipara*	Marsh-orchid, Northern	*Dactylorhiza purpurella*
Bitter-vetch	*Lathyrus linifolius*	Meadowsweet	*Filipendula ulmaria*
Bogbean	*Menyanthes trifoliata*	Milk-vetch, Purple	*Astragalus danicus*
Bog-myrtle	*Myrica gale*	Milkwort, Heath	*Polygala serpyllifolia*
Brooklime	*Veronica beccabunga*	Moor-grass, Purple	*Molinia caerulea*
Bugle	*Ajuga reptans*	Orchid, Fragrant	*Gymnadenia conopsea*
Buttercup, Meadow	*Ranunculus acris*	Orchid, Frog	*Coeloglossum viride*
Butterfly-orchid, Greater	*Platanthera chlorantha*	Orchid, Small-white	*Pseudorchis albida*
Butterwort, Common	*Pinguicula vulgaris*	Pansy, Mountain	*Viola lutea*
Cherry, Wild	*Prunus avium*	Pondweed, Bog	*Potamogeton polygonifolius*
Chickweed-wintergreen	*Trientalis europaea*	Primrose	*Primula vulgaris*
Cinquefoil, Marsh	*Potentilla palustris*	Quaking-grass	*Briza media*
Clover, Red	*Trifolium pratense*	Ragged-Robin,	*Lychnis flos-cuculi*
Clover, White	*Trifolium repens*	Rock-rose, Common	*Helianthemum nummularium*
Colt's-foot	*Tussilago farfara*	Rowan	*Sorbus aucuparia*
Cottongrass	*Eriophorum sp.*	Saxifrage. Purple	*Saxifraga oppositifolia*
Cowslip	*Primula veris*	Saxifrage, Yellow	*Saxifraga aizoides*
Crane's-bill, Wood	*Geranium sylvaticum*	Scabious, Devil's-bit	*Succisa pratensis*
Cuckooflower	*Cardamine pratensis*	Selfheal	*Prunella vulgaris*
Daisy	*Bellis perennis*	Sheep's-fescue, Viviparous	*Festuca vivipara*
Daisy, Oxeye	*Leucanthemum vulgare*	Sorrel, Common	*Rumex acetosa*
Deergrass	*Trichophorum cespitosum*		*subsp. acetosa*
Dog-rose	*Rosa canina*	Speedwell, Germander	*Veronica chamaedrys*
Dog-violet, Common	*Viola riviniana*	Speedwell, Heath	*Veronica officinalis*
Eyebright	*Euphrasia sp.*	Spotted-orchid, Common	*Dactylorhiza fuchsii*
Flax, Fairy	*Linum catharticum*	Spotted-orchid, Heath	*Dactylorhiza maculata*
Forget-me-not, Water	*Myosotis scorpioides*	St John's-wort, Slender	*Hypericum pulchrum*
Gentian, Field	*Gentianella campestris*	Strawberry, Wild	*Fragaria vesca*
Globeflower	*Trollius europaeus*	Sundew, Round-leaved	*Drosera rotundifolia*

Thistle, Marsh	*Cirsium palustre*	Vetchling, Meadow	*Lathyrus pratensis*
Thistle, Melancholy	*Cirsium heterophyllum*	Whin, Petty	*Genista anglica*
Thistle, Spear	*Cirsium vulgare*	Willow, Creeping	*Salix repens*
Thyme, Wild	*Thymus polytrichus*	Wintergreen, Common	*Pyrola minor*
Tormentil	*Potentilla erecta*	Wood-sorrel	*Oxalis acetosella*
Twayblade, Common	*Listera ovata*	Yarrow	*Achillea millefolium*
Vetch, Bush	*Vicia sepium*	Yellow-rattle	*Rhinanthus minor*
Vetch, Kidney	*Anthyllis vulneraria*	Yorkshire-fog	*Holcus lanatus*
Vetch, Tufted	*Vicia cracca*		

Total number of flowering plant species = 95, excluding Purple saxifrage which was not photographed on the meadow.

N.B. The above list should not be regarded as a formal botanical survey of plants on the meadow.

B) Scientific names for the flowering plant families encountered

The number of plant species represented in each family is shown in brackets

Bedstraw family (2)	Rubiaceae	Knotweed family (2)	Polygonaceae
Beech family (1)	Fagaceae	Lily family (2)	Liliaceae
Bellflower family (1)	Campanulaceae	Milkwort family (1)	Polygalaceae
Birch family (1)	Betulaceae	Orchid family (8)	Orchidaceae
Bladderwort family (2)	Lentibulariaceae	Pea family (9)	Fabaceae
Bogbean family (1)	Menyanthaceae	Pink family (1)	Caryophyllaceae
Bog myrtle family (1)	Myricaceae	Pondweed family (1)	Potamogetonaceae
Borage family (1)	Boraginaceae	Primrose family (3)	Primulaceae
Buttercup family (3)	Ranunculaceae	Rock rose family (1)	Cistaceae
Cabbage family (1)	Brassicaceae	Rose family (9)	Rosaceae
Crane's-bill family (1)	Geraniaceae	Saxifrage family (3)	Saxifragaceae
Daisy family (10)	Asteraceae	Sedge family (2)	Cyperaceae
Dead-nettle family (3)	Lamiaceae	St John's wort family (1)	Clusiaceae
Figwort family (8)	Scrophulariaceae	Sundew family (1)	Droseraceae
Fax family (1)	Linaceae	Teasel family (1)	Dipsacaceae
Gentian family (1)	Gentianaceae	Violet family (2)	Violaceae
Grass family (4)	Poaceae	Willow family (1)	Salicaceae
Heather family (5)	Ericaceae	Wood sorrel family (1)	Oxalidaceae

The total number of flowering plant families = 36

The vernacular names for flowering plant species have been taken from the 2007 data base list of English names provided by the Botanical Society of the British Isles. The scientific species names and the English and scientific family names are adopted from those used in the New English Flora by Clive Stace (second edition, 1997).

C) **Sources of Information**

I am deeply indebted to the many sources of information utilised in the preparation of text to accompany the photographs. This applies especially to those listed below, as well as to information lodged in my memory archive, but for which sources have become obscured with the passage of time.

Averis, A (2003) Springs and Flushes. Scottish Natural Heritage.
Alvin, KL (1997) The Observer's Book of Lichens. Frederick Warne.
Bailey, J (ed) (1999) Dictionary of Plant Sciences. Penguin.
Bee, J, Burton, J. Parks P & Whiteley et al (1974) The Oxford Book of Insects. Oxford University Press.
Brooks, M & Knight, C (1983) A Complete Guide to British Butterflies. Jonathan Cape Ltd.
Brooks, S & Lewington, R (1997) Field Guide to the Dragonflies and Damselflies of Great Britain and Ireland. British Wildlife Publishing.
Blamey, M, Fitter, R & Fitter A (2003) Wild Flowers of Britain and Ireland. A & C Black Publishers Ltd.
Corbet, GB & Andrews, IJ (2007) The Birds of Scotland. The Scottish Ornithologists' Club.
Gibbons, B & Brough, P (1996) The Hamlyn Photographic Guide to the Wild Flowers of Britain and Northern Europe. Chancellor Press.
Gilbert, O (2004) Lichens. Scottish Natural Heritage.
Haymann, P & Burton, P (1976) The Birdlife of Britain. Mitchell Beazley Publishers Ltd.
Lang, D (2004) Britain's Orchids. Wild*Guides* Ltd.
Lange, M & Hora, FB (1963) . Collins Guide to Mushrooms and Toadstools. Collins.
Mabberley, DJ (2009) Mabberley's Plant-Book. Cambridge University Press.
Macdonald, M (2003) Bumblebees. Scottish Natural Heritage.
MacKintosh, J, McCracken, D, Ford, M & Phillips D (2001) Managing Grasslands for Wildlife on Scottish Farms. Scottish Natural Heritage.
Mahon, A (1988) Grasshoppers and Bush Crickets of the British Isles. Shire Natural History.
Marshall, J & Ovenden, D A Guide to British grasshoppers and allied insects. FSC Publications.
Phillips, R (1980) Grasses, Ferns, Mosses & Lichens of Great Britain and Ireland. Pan Books Ltd.
Press, JR, Sutton, DA & Tebbs, BR et al (1981) Field Guide to the Wild Flowers of Britain. The Reader's Digest Association Ltd.
Raven, PH, Evert, RF & Eichhorn, SE (1992) Biology of Plants. Worth Publishers.
Scott, M (1995) Scottish Wildflowers. Harper Collins.
SNH, (1995) Boglands. Scottish Natural Heritage [author not credited].
Stace, C (2005) New Flora of the British Isles. Cambridge University Press.
Thain, M, & Hickman, M (1996) Dictionary of Biology. Penguin.
Thomas, JA (1986) RSNC Guide to Butterflies of the British Isles. Newnes Country Life Books.
Ward, S & MacKintosh, J (2001) Grasslands. Scottish Natural Heritage.
Waring, P, Townsend, M & Lewington, R (2003) Field Guide to the Moths of Great Britain and Ireland. British Wildlife Publishing.
Watling, R (2003) Fungi. Scottish Natural Heritage.